MacHaven

A Journey

MAURITA MOTLAND

ISBN 978-1-64191-071-2 (paperback)
ISBN 978-1-64191-072-9 (digital)

Christian Faith Publishing, Inc.
832 Park Avenue
Meadville, PA 16335
www.christianfaithpublishing.com

Printed in the United States of America

In memory of Jerry Thompson, who, upon meeting Mac, told us, "You know this is not a Labrador, this is a 'Love-ador.'"

Introduction

Over twelve years ago, we brought home our lovable bundle of yellow fur, Mac. As we cuddled him, trained him, and played with this little pup, we had no idea about the new world that was to be opened before us: the world of the working Labrador retriever. We, of course, fell in love with Mac but also the breed. Labrador retrievers are awesome dogs, and I love watching them work. Whether it's hunting, search and rescue, being a service dog, I love to watch them perform. They are even being trained to alert their owner of medical conditions. That is amazing to me. They are fun, versatile dogs. They love to work, but they'll also hang out with you and lie around with you. I enjoy taking pictures of them, and for some reason, I think I could sell books of all the pictures I've taken of my Labradors, even though they are not professional. I'm in love. Talk to me about your kids, and I'll talk to you about my Labradors. I won't skip a beat, and it will relate. Really! Friends and family will confirm this.

I never thought having a dog would stretch me in personal development. But it has. I've read more books about training dogs for general obedience and for hunting than I've read for personal development. I am a Cesar Millan *Dog Whisperer* fan. I continually strive to be my dogs' calm, assertive pack leader. I'm continually amazed at how long it's taking me and how much focus and energy it takes. I'm seeing improvement, but it seems like I should have things figured out a lot better by now. It's been over thirteen years! I used to think I was patient, confident, and giving. My dogs show me daily who I really am and the work I have to do. Yet they want to be with me and are always happy to see me. And that is amazing and makes me happy.

CHAPTER 1

How It Began

I closed my eyes and took a deep breath. The sun felt so wonderful, warming my face as I looked upward to soak it up. I sank deeper into my coat. The gentle splashing of the duck decoy bouncing on the waves lulled me into a peaceful place. I love it when the sun comes out to play. *Bang!* My thoughts were intruded by my brother, Russ, shooting. "Where'd he come from?" I blurted out, a bit embarrassed that I hadn't seen him.

"He came in low."

"Nice shot, Russ."

Mike came out of the reeds and patted Russ on the shoulder. "Well, you better go get him before more come in."

Russ grabbed the net and tried to hand it to Mike. "It's your turn, isn't it?"

"It's your bird!" Mike shoved Russ toward the lake.

"Okay, okay. Don't push me into the water!" Russ made his way down to the water with a big smile. Each step was slow and deliberate as he pulled his feet up out of the mucky bottom of Linda Lake. "A retriever sure would be nice." Russ gave Mike a glance.

"You're the one with the bird dog," Mike blurted back. "Shannon's an upland bird dog, not a waterfowl dog. Isn't it time for you and Rita to get a dog? They'd be good for finding the ones that fall in the reeds too."

"Yeah, upland is right," Mike sparred back. "Shannon wouldn't walk across a two-inch creek!"

"Hey, be nice now." Russ smiled as he continued to make his way, slow and deliberate, toward his duck. I stood up to stretch and soak up some more sun. A Labrador retriever. Yes, a puppy might be in our near future.

CHAPTER 2

The First Dog

My husband, Mike, and I both grew up having cats and dogs in the family. We rarely took our pets out in public and rarely demanded more of them then to play, not pee in the house and not chew up the furniture. When we got married, we were totally happy without pets for the first five to six years. Then we both started thinking about getting a dog. We heard that a friend was looking for a home for one of her dogs, an American Eskimo named Chelsea. She was about six years old, potty-trained and well-behaved. Perfect. With both of us working full-time, we couldn't see potty training a puppy.

We had a lot of fun with her. She was an awesome companion. We took her everywhere. Chelsea was about twelve years old when my brother introduced us to waterfowl and upland bird hunting. We already hunted deer and elk; now we had a new vice. My brother had a Brittany spaniel, Shannon. Great for upland bird hunting, but not much help with waterfowl. So after a couple of seasons of Mike and my brother wading in muddy lakes out to their chests to retrieve our birds and losing a number of winged birds, Mike suggested we get a Labrador retriever. So I got a list of breeders from a coworker's wife who trained dogs, and I contacted each of them. It was important to us that the breeder hunt with their dogs. We didn't want just a show dog, but we did want the classic Labrador retriever look. After speaking with several from the list, we found one we felt comfortable with. As chance had it, there was a litter due in September, just weeks away. We made our deposit and hoped for a yellow female Labrador to be born in their next litter.

Yes, female. After observing male dogs, we decided we wanted a female. Males seem to pee all over everything. And yellow, to blend in with the cattails where we hunt. We anxiously awaited the news of color and gender available. Meanwhile, what would we name our puppy? I began searching the internet for the most common names as we wanted to avoid those. Our plan was to register her also. So you have the registered name and the call name. I wanted something catchy and fun, like Clovercreek Annie Get Your Gun (the breeder is always part of the registered name). Call name, Annie, or Chablais Singing in the Rain. Call name, Tenor. But the call name is important because that's what you call her every day. That's the bonding name. We decided we'd start there. We had a list of several we were considering as we waited for the news of color and gender available.

On September 26, eight puppies were born, six black and two yellow. Both of the yellows were male. How bad do we want the puppy now? Do we wait for another litter? Should we consider a black one? Check other breeders? Mike was not about to spend another bird season retrieving our birds in the muck at Linda Lake, so a male it is. The breeders assured us that he could be trained as to where it is acceptable to pee. They also pointed out that females are referred to as bitches in the dog world, and there's a reason for that. After some discussion, we let the breeders choose which of the two yellow males would be best suited for the role he was to play in our life, family member and hunter.

It wasn't until we were driving out to the breeders to see our puppy for the first time that we decided on his name. As we drove through Machias, a little berg on the way to the breeder's home, Mike said, "Machias. That's a connection of where he was born. His call name could be Mac, that's a short name for Machias."

I thought about it. "So Hiltonhall's Machias? It needs a little more. How about Burton? My dad's middle name was Burton. How about Hiltonhall's Machias Burton, call name Mac?" Mike liked it. It was decided. My father had died during my senior year of high school. Later, I told my mom about the honor we'd given Dad with his middle name being part of Mac's registered name. She laughed. I guess she didn't see it as an honor like we did.

Mac and his littermates.

CHAPTER 3

Welcome Home, Mac

Mac wasn't ready to come home on our first visit. He wasn't ready to leave his mom yet. Due to that fact and then hunting season for deer and elk followed, we weren't able to bring Mac home until Thanksgiving weekend. Mac was nine weeks old then. We assured Chelsea that we wouldn't let him bother her (she was about fourteen years old). We bought Mac a bed and a purple collar (that was the color of his puppy ribbon that the breeders used to identify him). We'd wait for food until we got directives on his diet from the breeders. We were very excited to go get Mac. We'd been planning and looking forward to this event for over a month.

We put Mac's bed in the back seat of the Explorer. Chelsea sat in my lap. It was a beautiful drive to where the breeders live. It took just over an hour, and today that was way too long. Finally, we arrived. Chuck and Sharon Hilton greeted us and ushered us in to their dining room. The entry opened to the living room and dining room. Their home was comfortable and was tastefully decorated with a Labrador and bird-hunting theme. They had us take a seat at their dining room table and brought in a stack of papers along with a bag of dog food.

I started to get impatient. Where's our puppy? Where's Mac? "Okay, we just have to go over a few things with you before you take

Mac home." Yes, they already knew about Mac's name. They had asked us so they could start calling him by his name. They were very sweet and kind about everything. They explained about registering him, how to fill out the papers, and when they needed to be turned in. Then we discussed his vaccinations and food and signed an agreement that if we couldn't take care of Mac any longer, no questions asked, we were to return him to them. Are we done yet?

Finally, with all that out of the way, we got to see Mac. Mike took our bag of goodies for Mac and put it in the back of the car. The Hiltons led us to an enclosed area in their garage. A radio hung on the plywood wall with country music playing softly. Three puppies were further confined with a shorter piece of plywood secured to the walls, creating a pen. There was sawdust on the ground, and the puppies were huddled together in a corner but quickly got up and ran to greet us, jumping up on the plywood and wagging their tails. Chuck stepped over the wall and grabbed Mac. Supporting him with both hands, he gave him to me. I took him in my arms and snuggled him in tight. He snuggled in too. Oh, my sweet bundle of fur. It was love at first hug. We fussed over him and took pictures of us holding him and then of the Hiltons. Then we loaded him up and thanked the Hiltons. I sat in back to keep Mac in his bed for the ride home. Chelsea sat in the front next to Mike, showing little interest in the new puppy in the back. The ride home was much shorter than the ride out.

We decided Mac was going to sleep in "his room," our downstairs bathroom. We set up a nice bed and a potty box. The potty box was a woodbox Mike built, about three by four feet, which had wood pellets in it. Like a cat box, but for a puppy. This was a suggestion from Chuck Hilton. We had an adjustable gate we put at the door. I thought shutting the door would make him feel boxed in and less likely to relax. We also had a radio to keep him company. "Good night, Mac! Sleep well." Upstairs we went to our bedroom along with Chelsea. Chelsea slept with us in our bedroom and had done so since we first got her. That was her norm, and we wanted to give her space from Mac. Mac, however, was not happy about this arrangement and protested. We knew he would bark but hoped he would eventually stop and we could all get some sleep. Apparently we didn't have the gate quite figured out, and Mac was able to knock it over. He sat at the bottom of the stairs, whining and barking. He hadn't experienced stairs yet, so he didn't attempt the climb. I was too tired to figure the gate out, so I put a chair in front of the gate. Mac was very persistent, and we didn't get much sleep that night.

The second night should be better. Right? We put Mac to bed, gave him loves, and headed up to bed. We got all snuggled into bed, and no barking. Silence. I snuggled into my pillow, thinking, *Maybe we'll get some sleep tonight.*

"What's that at the door?" Mike muttered as he rolled over. I reluctantly got up and opened the door. There was Mac, so happy as only a puppy can be. He had figured out how to get up the stairs. I guess we still didn't get that gate to work properly. Okay. So he wanted to be with his pack. Right? The next day, we bought a wire crate for his bed, and guess where Mac slept the following night and to this day. Yup, in the bedroom with the rest of his pack.

As a further welcome to Mac, my friends gave us a puppy shower. Okay, it was really more for me. Due to timing issues with meeting the man of my dreams (Mike), I'd never had any children. Consequently, I never had a baby shower. So my wonderful friends decided I needed a puppy shower. It was great fun: decorations, a cake with a picture of a Lab puppy on it, and of course, gifts. I couldn't believe all the toys Mac got. And the attention? Mac was in heaven. My friends had a lot of fun with Mac. Maybe this party was really for them? After all the fun and excitement, after the last guest left, we headed to bed. The routine was to take the dogs out before, but where was Mac? This party was more than a baby boy could take. He was sound asleep in his room, on the cool floor by the toilet.

CHAPTER 4

The Next Era

Chelsea was about fourteen years old when we brought Mac home. She weighed eighteen pounds. Mac, at nine weeks, weighed nineteen pounds and was still growing. My brother, Russ, called him butterball. He was a wonderful, cuddly ball of fur—a very playful ball of fur—maybe even at times mischievous. I tried to work with him to respect Chelsea and give her space. Mac just wanted to play with her. As Chelsea walked by, he'd recoil just slightly and then pounce, tumbling Chelsea over. She was such a sweet girl. She never snapped at him, although he probably needed her to do it.

Now began the new routine for potty training the puppy. Keeping a routine was helpful. Their little bladders can only hold for so long. So we (mostly me) were up in the middle of the night for a while. I didn't mind too much as Mac was really snuggly after sleeping. I was working part-time, and Mike had a construction business. We tried to minimize the time Mac would be alone. I would leave later in the morning, and Mike would come home at lunch and would be home an hour before me in the evening. We still used the downstairs bathroom for Mac when we had to leave him at home. We finally figured out how to work the gate, and Mac had a cozy home in our downstairs bathroom. We had a radio set up just like he was used to at the breeders, and he would get a hidden treat in a toy before we left. That probably kept him busy for maybe an hour. We had to remember to put the toilet paper up when leaving in the morning. I call this puppy-proofing the room. Mac loved toilet paper. If we forgot to put it out of his reach, he would keep busy for a while, shredding it and getting it all off the roll. I just wasn't sure that if he ingested some of that toilet paper, that would be the best for him. We did forget a time or two and came home to find the whole roll shredded all over the floor. He was always very proud of his work and showed no remorse.

After the morning routine of going outside, eating, and going outside again, there was playing. Puppy needs his exercise. Next was the challenge to get ready for work in a timely manner. So you brush your teeth, wash your face, and then play with Mac. He was just so cute and kind of hard to ignore when he was tugging on your bathrobe. "Okay, Mac. I got to get dressed now." Mac followed me over to the drawer where my socks are. I opened the drawer, and Mac bounced over and snatched a pair of my socks. "Mac! Fetch 'em here. Fetch my socks here!" (You never want to discourage a retriever from retrieving. If he has something in his mouth he shouldn't, like my socks, take the opportunity to train. Have him fetch it to you.) Before you leave, potty the dogs, cuddle Chelsea, play with Mac more, put Mac in his room, give him his puzzle treat, pick up the toilet paper roll, turn his radio on, and snuggle Chelsea again. Late for work again!

Gradually we allowed Mac more access to the rest of the house when home alone. Before leaving, I'd walk around and make certain to puppy-proof the area. Occasionally books or magazines would be left within reach, and we'd come home to chewed-up remains. Oh, and the TV remote. I think we went through two of those during Mac's puppyhood. Then there was the first time we left him with Mike's son, Jason, for a few days. I think we lost one of the remotes during that venture, and Mac tore the carpet up by the front-door entry. He pulled the carpet up at the corner and then chewed some of the padding beneath. We were able to put the carpet back, but there was a little hole in the padding that perhaps only we noticed.

Mac was about four months old when we noticed Chelsea starting to lose strength. She wasn't eating well and was having frequent accidents in the house. There were a couple of times in the last two years when we had to take her to the vet because she wasn't eating. They kept her for a couple of days, feeding her intravenously. She revived both of those times. This time wasn't looking too good. I cooked chicken for her every day as that's the only thing I could get her to eat. I would hold her in my lap while sitting on the couch and feed her chicken by hand. Mac would drool as he sat watching us, hoping he would get some of that chicken. And of course, he would.

Chelsea was eating less and less in spite of my efforts. We came to the very difficult decision to have Chelsea put to sleep. Her quality of life had declined drastically in the last few weeks. We took her to the vet with heavy hearts. I felt sick to my stomach. We cried as the vet checked Chelsea and inserted the catheter. The vet left us alone for a while as we held her and cried. We continued to hold her as they administered the drug. It was the hardest thing we've ever done. We cried the rest of the day. As I would take Mac outside, I'd see Chelsea's noseprints on the sliding glass door. A knot would form in my throat, but I had to focus on Mac. He needed me. It was weeks before I could wash the sliding glass door or the windows inside our Ford Explorer as I didn't want to wash off her noseprints.

Now my attention and affections were solely on Mac. And he kept us busy and thoroughly entertained. Once at the family cabin, Mike, my mother-in-law, Grace, and I were relaxing around the table, talking about an earlier drive we had taken and the deer and elk we had seen. Our conversation was interrupted by repeated clanging of Mac's metal food dish as he pushed it down the hall on the laminate flooring, his face covered by the dish. He'd trip and roll over the bowl then circle around and do it again. After a good belly laugh, I picked him up. "I guess someone thinks it's dinnertime." I pulled him up and gave him a big kiss on his nose. "Such a kissable face. I can hardly stand it." He wagged his tail and attempted a kiss back.

When working out in the yard, we would secure Mac's retractable leash to a deck rail post then attached it to his collar. He would start exploring, and pretty soon he'd be wrapped around a bush. He'd whimper, and I'd have to untangle him. I would detach the leash, and he would try to play with me as I would untangle the leash. "Okay, let's see if you'll stay close if I don't attach you to the leash." I kept an eye on him as I went back to weeding. He watched me a bit then started sniffing his leash. I heard him barking and looked to see him pulling the retractable leash out, then he'd let it go and chase after it barking. Then he'd pull it out and chase after it again. He found a job. He was a happy boy.

We began calling ourselves Pappa and Momma for Mac's sake. If I was home with Mac and Mike arrived from working or from running an errand, I'd see his truck pulling in and say, "Pappa's home! Let's go get Pappa!" Mac would perk up and follow me to go greet Mike. On the weekend mornings when we slept in a bit and had more leisure time, Mike would pull the sheet up over his head, and I'd call to Mac, "Where's Pappa? Mac, where's Pappa?" He would pile up on Mike's chest and nose at Mike's face. Sometimes I'd help and pull the sheet down a little, and Mac would nuzzle in and give Mike big puppy kisses. Mac loved this game.

Mac, proud of his toilet paper work.

CHAPTER 5

Beyond Basic Training

The breeders recommended taking Mac to a professional trainer when he was one year old to begin his training to hunt. The professional would then keep Mac about one month. The length of time might vary with each dog and the professional. Meanwhile, we began working on basic obedience, getting him used to a collar and lead, and crate training. We bought a crate that he would fit when fully grown then put a box in the back of it to create a space for his current size. This gave him just the right amount of room to stand and curl up, nice and cozy. I introduced him to it with treats and followed the instructions that came with the crate. I began feeding his regular meals in the crate too. I could still see that happy boy on a full-out run to that crate, and then he'd take a flying leap inside. He loved his meals, very food motivated.

Mac was now six months old, and we were walking him every morning on his leash. There was a small park about a block from our home that we could work with him off leash. Rain or sunshine, we were committed to walk and work with our boy. Mac was not lifting his leg yet as he peed. Yes, this was a concern for us. Shouldn't he be lifting his leg? The neighbor's dog was full-grown, and he still didn't lift his leg. Isn't this a sign of him being a strong, confident dog? Each morning, on our walk and every time we took him out to do his business, we watched. Today? Will it be today? Yes, these were the people who wanted a female because males pee everywhere.

It was a mild winter morning, and it wasn't raining. You can't ask for much more from a northwest winter morning. We geared up and headed out for the walk to the park. We crossed the street and headed up the hill, just like every morning. It was still dark, and you could see our breath, even Mac's, as we pushed up the hill. We approached the stretch where every dog in the neighborhood must leave his mark as Mac was always attentive to this area. My mind was on my day ahead; payroll needed to go out today. Wait, did that just happen? I gave Mike's arm a jab with my elbow. "Did you see that? He lifted his leg!" We both smiled and nodded with satisfaction. Our boy lifted his leg! It's like the baby's first steps.

I began reading books on training hunting dogs. I started with the ones recommended by the Hiltons and then other ones we found online. I began thinking that maybe we should be the ones who trained Mac for hunting. It's a great bonding experience to work and train your dog. So I began looking for a professional who would train us to train Mac. I found one through friends at work who had worked with them to train their dog.

When Mac was eight months old, we took him to meet our trainer, Linda Burns. We were to meet at Safeway in the parking lot and then follow her to nearby fields. As we pulled into the Safeway parking lot, a somewhat petite lady wearing a baseball cap, camo jacket, tight jeans, and riding boots flagged us to where she stood by her truck.

"Linda?"

"Yes, that's me." Linda came confidently toward our vehicle, which had pulled in next to hers. I opened the door slightly, and Mac stood across my lap, excited to meet this new person. "Are you just a bad boy? Oh, what a bad boy you are!" Linda's lilting voice made Mac wiggle and wag his tail.

He's not a bad boy, I thought, feeling slightly defensive.

"Follow me." Linda turned sharply and waved her arm as she jumped into her truck. "We'll head to the fields just a couple miles from here."

I had a few tools necessary for training hunting dogs that the many books I had read suggested: a collar and leash (the obvious ones) and a thirty-foot check cord. Oh yes, and the whistle. We pulled in to the parking area by the fields, next to Linda's truck. As we all piled out of our vehicles, Linda hollered, "Let's first take a walk." She walked to the back of her truck, opened the back, and pulled out this heavy-duty drawer. I thought I had dog tools. "Do you have a check cord?" she asked as she rummaged through this drawer. I meekly showed her the cord. "That will do. Let's check this collar you have." Linda kneeled in front of Mac, grabbed his collar, and slid her fingers inside between the collar and his neck. "This will work. Put that cord on the boy. Hold it loose. If he pulls, give it a slight tug like this and say, 'Don't pull.'" Linda demonstrated a tug out to the side of Mac's neck. So off we went, with Linda giving pointers and tips. We came upon some fencing, half of which was broken and leaning. One post had barbed wire wrapped around the top. Mac started barking. "What is it, boy?" Linda looked toward Mac and then in the direction he was looking. "What, you don't like that barbwire? It's okay. Leave it." And she motioned us all to continue the walk. Mac was in heaven, running ahead and bounding through the tall grass. Every little bit, he'd look back at us. "Good checking in, Mac!" she hollered out to Mac. Then she turned to us. "He has a natural tendency to check in. That's good."

As we circled back to the trucks, we passed a small pool in the creek. Linda had us pause, and she watched Mac. Mac sniffed a bit at the water but moved on by it. "What? Haven't you had him in water yet?"

"There isn't any water around our home to take him to," I defensively explained. I had taken him into a swimming pool when he was about three months old. He wasn't able to touch ground anywhere and was not happy when I held him in the water. Other than puddles, that was his only water experience. Linda continued, "You put your boots on, and you walk him through puddles, any kind of water. He should have been introduced to water by now." I felt like quite the neglecting mother. So began the training sessions for Mac and me with Linda. We met with her once a week for the summer, working to get Mac ready for the fall hunting season. On our second meeting, Linda brought her adult Lab, Tex, who led Mac right away into the water, and just like that, he was swimming. Yeah!

Our training involved lots of runs for bumpers and an occasional bird as we got close to the hunting season. Linda tried to give us as many scenarios as possible that we'd face on our first hunt with Mac. "Merriatta, take Mac up on the mound, and we'll throw the bumpers on the land just across the water," Linda hollered as she walked to her position to toss the bumpers. I'm not certain when it started, but she somehow started calling me by a name that was kind of close to my name but not. Since it was always while we were working in the field and others were with us, I didn't feel right hollering back "It's Maurita!" So Merriatta it was for a while. I e-mailed her once, explaining it's like saying "more of Rita" without saying the *of*. But that did not work. Finally, one of her friends who had been working with us figured it out and asked me about it. He must have told her as the next week I heard "Maurita" hollered across the field.

September was finally here, and hunting would begin in October. We arranged with Linda to do a hunt at Cooke Canyon. Cooke Canyon is a great place to take inexperienced young dogs. It is privately owned, and they raise pheasant, quail, and chukars for the hunt. We arranged for six pheasant hens as the roosters could potentially hurt a young dog with their spurs. Linda then planted one bird and flagged us to start the hunt with Mac. We knew approximately where the bird was, but Mac did not. Mac was excited to be out in the fields, and he was working, running between Mike and me with his nose to the ground. Then his tail went straight; he stopped and then pushed into the brush. Up flew the pheasant, wings flapping, and *bang*, Mike got it. Mac knew what to do. He got in the brush and retrieved the hen. "Good boy! Ha ha! Mac's first bird." Mike held it out for all to see. Mike handed it to me, and Mac watched as I put it in Mike's hunting vest. Mac now had a prance and was holding his head up as we walked to our next spot to plant a bird. Linda smiled and nudged me. "Look at him. He's so proud."

Yeah, he's a good boy, I thought and smiled as I watched him prance along with attitude.

Mac gained confidence with each bird. He found them all and did not need any help. It was a beautiful sunny day in eastern Washington, and we were feeling successful. It was Mac's birthday too. He turned one year old. We celebrated with Linda at Cooke Canyon with cupcakes and a balloon. Mac couldn't eat the cupcakes, but his birthday celebration was the hunt, and he was a very happy boy. He slept well during the two-hour truck ride home.

CHAPTER 6

The Real Thing

Waterfowl hunting opened in October, and our first hunt of the season would be at Linda Lake with Russ. We really hadn't talked much about sitting in a duck blind during our training. Do I hold on to Mac's collar? Then I can't shoot. What if he breaks out and someone accidently shoots him? I was feeling a little nervous about this first duck hunt. I sent Linda an e-mail with my concerns. She replied to secure him to a stake in the blind on a short lead. Then he wouldn't break, scare the ducks, and cause problems. We got him a neoprene vest to wear in the blind and for swimming to help keep him warm. It provided some buoyancy, but not much. We also threw in an extra coat to throw over him to keep him warm in the blind.

The day arrived for the first waterfowl hunt. We were to meet Russ at 4:00 a.m. in the park 'n ride just off I-90. It was misting and really dark! "Load up, Mac!" Mac happily jumped into the front seat between Mike and me. Mike and I climbed in and buckled up. Mac plopped down on my lap. "You stinker." I pulled him in for a snuggle. "You have no idea of the adventure yet ahead." I rubbed his tummy and took a sip of coffee from my traveler cup. There's nothing better than a furry lap warmer for these early cold mornings.

Russ was waiting for us as we arrived at the park 'n ride. Not too many cars in the lot, so his red work truck was easy to spot. We loaded him and his stuff up then continued the three-hour drive east to Linda Lake. It was still dark when we arrived at Linda Lake, but the sun was just peeking over the hilltops. Since this is public hunting, there is often competition for the blinds on the lake. "Looking good. I don't see any other vehicles," Russ announced as we pulled in to the designated parking area.

I reluctantly left my cozy place in the truck to get ready. Mac tried to follow. "You've got to stay in here yet, buddy." Mac licked my face, wagging his tail, looking for an opportunity to escape.

Gearing up in twenty-degree weather is not my favorite part of duck hunting. You have to take off your jeans and put on your waders, which is often a struggle. All this exposes you to the elements. Your fingers are getting numb as all the things you touch are very cold, and you can't do these things with gloves on. I don't know if this is fact, but the dry atmosphere east of the mountains makes twenty degrees even colder. Motivated by the adventure ahead, I pushed on. I was excited for Mac's first duck hunt—waders on, coat liner on, coat on, gloves in pocket, hand warmers in pocket, headlamp on, hat on over headlamp, bucket to sit on was ready, gun was out and ready. Mike and Russ were struggling with their decoy bags. They each carried a large decoy bag on their backs that holds approximately twelve decoys each. I lifted up each bag so they can adjust the straps over their shoulders and around their waists. "Are we ready?" Mike and Russ each gave a nod. "Okay, Mac. Come on!" Mac jumped out as soon as the door was opened, and he was busy right away checking everything out. Mike locked the truck, and we were off.

The terrain surrounding Linda Lake varied from batches of cattails to larger stretches of sage and clumps of tall grass. I don't know the name of this grass, but this clump of grass is three to four feet tall and is in a clump about six to twelve inches in circumference. The clumps are three to four inches apart. This creates a very uneven terrain and is particularly difficult to maneuver over and through in the dark. The grass is a blue-yellow color and rather spiky. The added challenge is moving over this terrain in waders. Walking in waders is like having a huge, thick rubber band wrapped around the middle of your thighs. You have to work for every step you take. Loaded down with all the gear, we were pushing as fast as we can to make sure we get to our spot before anyone else does.

Mac, totally unaware of our struggles, ran and leaped over the obstacles back and forth between us all, way out ahead of Russ, who usually leads with his long legs, then back to check on Mike and me. My sweet husband always keeps a slower pace for my sake. Finally, after what seemed like an hour, the cove we like to set up on was in sight. And it was open! No one was there!

We all plopped our gear down, and the boys started setting up the decoys. Mac stuck his nose into every hole he could find in the cattails. Then he was into the water to check on the boys. I set up our buckets and guns in two of the blinds made in the cattails. I love the sky at this time. It was still mostly dark, but the sun was just peeking over the horizon with bright orange streaking out across the sky. Mac and I settle into our blind, me on my bucket and Mac sitting in front of me, watching intently as the boys finish with the decoys and climb into their blinds. Mac is very serious when he hunts. He doesn't like me fussing with him as I sometimes do. Now we're on the ready. Just need some ducks to come in, or a goose. One of the things we like about Linda Lake is that geese fly in also. Most waterfowl hunting, you're hunting either ducks or geese but rarely both. Now, they don't always cooperate. That's why it's called hunting. We were hoping they'll cooperate today. And now, we have a bird dog that will retrieve them for us. Oh, happy day!

It was a beautiful, crisp day and a little hazy with some sunbreaks. About a couple of hundred feet or so from the shoreline, the water was frozen. We all got some ducks in the morning hunt, and Mac was stellar. We, of course, had to take pictures of his first duck and the second and the third. We'd give him the duck to hold for the picture, and Mac would then prance around with it, showing it off. After a few attempts, we did get some good pictures.

After lunch break and a cigar, we settled in for the afternoon hunt. Now is when the geese start flying in. First thing in the morning, they lift off the lake and go to the fields for feeding. Then they return to the lake in the afternoon and spend the evening on the lake. We all watched the sky in anticipation. As expected, a small group flew over our decoys. They passed over but then circled back. Yes! They were coming in. Wait now. They locked their wings to land in the decoys, and we all jumped up. Mac was barking and tugging at his lead: "Let me out, let me out!" Mike and Russ each got one down, and Russ winged a third. I let Mac off, and he jumped into the water after the downed geese.

This was Mac's first retrieve for a goose. A goose is two to three times bigger than a duck or pheasant. I was a little concerned as to how he might react. We've sat in blinds in the past watching other hunters across the lake become exasperated trying to get their Lab to get out and retrieve the goose. Mac knew his job and, without hesitation, grabbed that first goose and brought it to Mike. Then out for the second. *Piece of cake, Mom. What's your concern?* The celebration had to wait, as the winged goose swam out to the edge of the ice. Mac did not see this third bird, and we were about to send Mac out on a long swim for something he did not see. This is called a blind retrieve. You line the dog up and send him out with a command. This is an advanced situation, something Mac had not really been trained at. I lined Mac up and gave the command "Back!" He looked at me then looked out at the water and then back at me. He looked out at the water as I gave the command again, and just at that moment, the goose flopped up onto the ice. Mac saw it, and off he went.

"Attaboy!" Wow, that was a far swim. My mind was reeling as I watched Mac swim out to the bird. Is that normal? Can all water dogs swim that far? What if he gets to it but can't make it back? Those geese are almost as big as him. Mac was swimming strong and with confidence. He got the bird! "Attaboy!" We all clapped and hooted. "Here, Mac!" I followed with the whistle command. Linda Lake is shallow—well, waist-deep for my brother, who is six foot four. "Russ, could you wade out in case he needs aid in coming back in?" I have a wonderful brother. He sludged his way out as Mac swam in. Russ got as far out as he could without filling his waders, holding his gun up. Mac came in with the goose and swam right past Russ, barely giving him a glance. "Woo-hoo, Mac! Good boy!" We couldn't give him enough praise. We took a picture of him holding the goose. You can see Mac's head, eyes, nose, and feet. The goose's body covered the rest of him. That was a great end to a good day at Linda Lake and Mac's first waterfowl hunt.

CHAPTER 7

Being the Pack Leader

We got a few more hunts in before the season ended. It's never as much as you'd like. Work and, sometimes, the weather make it difficult. Mac grew more confident with each hunt. He would sit in the blind next to me, eyes focused on the skyline, with his tail wagging contently. That is such a peaceful time for me. I love sitting in a blind with my dog. They're happy to be there with you; the beauty of nature surrounds you, and there is peace.

I decided to continue training with Linda after hunting season ended. There was so much to learn, and I felt we'd barely touched on it. I had chosen to cut my hours back at work so I could help with Mike's construction company more. This also afforded time once a week for training Mac. Every Monday, Mac and I would head north to meet Linda for a couple of hours of fieldwork. On the days I worked, I was able to take Mac with me. I worked at a shipyard, and the owner loved Mac. Mac always put him in a good mood, and that made everybody's mood better. Everybody loved Mac, well almost. There was a lady who was helping her daughter in the office down the hall. She was deathly afraid of dogs from an earlier experience in life. Mac sensed this fear and figured something was wrong. She would duck into closets or frantically run down the hall into her office. Mac would bark at her but never chased her. Her daughter tried to talk to her about being confident and ignoring Mac, but she wouldn't do it. Luckily, she wasn't there too often, and when she was, I made sure Mac stayed next to me.

During lunch breaks, Mac and I would practice our walk. We needed a lot of practice. Mac wanted to be out front like when we're hunting, which meant pulling on the leash. I tried all the tools and the techniques, prong collars, tapping his chest with my foot. Nothing seemed to work, but we kept practicing. I said "heel" a lot. The shipyard was in an industrial area with other office buildings and next to railroad tracks, so our walk involved walking along the tracks at times. One day, we were several blocks from the office walking along the tracks when I noticed another lady coming out of another building, walking her dog. He was a rather large dog, a bit bigger than Mac. When he saw us, he tugged hard on the leash; it let loose, and he was on a dead run toward us. I stood tall with Mac by my side, thinking, *He looks mostly excited, not vicious.* I took a deep breath and planted my feet. *I am a strong pack leader*, I encouraged myself. As the dog approached, Mac pulled out ahead of me, also being pack leader (not good). He barked and growled, and in my effort to keep him at bay and away from the other dog, I wrapped the leash around my legs, and I found myself on the ground surrounded by the two dogs. I reached up and grabbed the collar of the other dog, and all was calm. I was working on untangling myself and getting up as the lady ran up to us apologizing. "I'm so sorry. He's not my dog. He's my friend's. Are you okay?" I brushed myself off as she took her friend's dog and attached his leash. I briefly scanned myself and Mac. "We're okay."

"Are you sure? The clip must not have attached to his collar."

"It's okay, really." Mac and I continued our walk back to the office as the lady walked with her friend's dog in the other direction. As we walked back, Mac sniffed and explored as if nothing had happened. I was a bit sore where I landed on my hip, but my ego was probably more bruised. "What a pack leader I was," I said quietly to Mac. "I hope you'll be patient with me, Mac. I have lots of work to do."

Calm and assertive, that's what a pack leader is supposed to be. Mike and I are to be Mac's pack leaders. We mostly have it. We can take his food, toys, and bones away. He does all the commands like "sit," "here," "stay" … well, maybe not "stay" so well. It's mostly the walk. We kept practicing. Maybe some of it was because when he's hunting, he's out ahead of us. At one point in our training sessions, Linda hollered, "Maurita, you've got to butch up!" Butch up? What does that mean, really? Getting the right picture of what the pack leader is has taken a long time for me. It's not forceful. It's actually caring, confident, and strong. Dominant, pushy people who are only concerned about their agenda and don't care if they're making everyone miserable are not the right image of what the pack leader is. So here is my journey with Mac, becoming his caring, confident, and strong pack leader.

Mac was the perfect dog for us. He didn't mind that I hadn't quite figured these things out. He loved to hunt, train, swim, play, and go everywhere with me. When working drills and I didn't give him enough time to respond to the "sit" whistle, I became anxious and hollered "sit" at him in frustration, then he would sit, smile at me, and wag his tail. He was saying, "It's okay, Mom, I got this. Trust me." The smile with tail wag would always melt me. I'd smile too. Then we'd try again and get it eventually.

CHAPTER 8

Breeding—the Question

September arrived again, Mac turned two years old, and hunting season was just a month away. We met with Linda at Cooke Canyon to let Mac brush up on his hunting skills. I love September. The days are sunny and warm, but the evenings are cool. This was a beautiful September day. Mac was hunting hard in front of us as we pushed through the tall brown grass. Linda walked up next to me and gave me a nudge as we were watching Mac. "Mac is a gorgeous boy. You should consider breeding him."

My eyes lit up. *Breed him?* I thought. When we started this whole thing with Mac, we were happy if Mac was able to find the bird and bring it to us. I lovingly watched Mac. A Mac puppy would be awesome. He is such a wonderful dog. I became enamored with this idea. But hunting season first. We'll have to think about it later.

This year proved to be a great hunting season. Mike and I both got an elk. The bird season was great too, and Mac continued to be the best dog ever. Everything came to a close at the end of January as with every year. We just couldn't say goodbye, though, so we decided to go to Cooke Canyon as it was open for hunting through February. Russ also wanted to give Shannon another day of hunting, so we set up for a hunt on the second Saturday in February.

It was a bright, sunny day and a crisp thirty-two degrees. There were still patches of snow on the ground. The dogs were pacing and chattering as we got our guns and ammunition out. We were going to do some target shooting first, so the dogs were secured to the back end of the truck on long leads. The dogs could hardly contain themselves with the shooting and didn't understand why they couldn't go fetch the birds. After an hour of practice shooting, it was time to set out on the hunt. The birds had been planted, and the dogs were past ready.

The area we were hunting was a wide-open field of grass. They had placed dead Christmas trees throughout to produce brush for the birds. The bird would be placed in the cover of the Christmas tree, and the tree was flagged, so we knew where the bird was placed, but not the dog. This works most of the time, but sometimes the bird wanders off. Then it's still out there, and the dog should still be able to find it. The wind was perfect, and the dogs were catching the sent. Mac was in heaven, running back and forth with his nose to the ground. The dogs had found all the birds, but we (the shooters) had missed a few. So we wanted to circle around where we had seen them land. After a brief break while we discussed our plan, we took off. We hadn't gone far when Mac's back legs started wobbling and going out under him. He kept trying to go and wasn't going to stop. "Mike, something's wrong with Mac!" I ran to Mac, set my gun down, and took hold of his collar. Mac was panting hard and resisting my hold a little. "We better give him a break and get him some water," Mike spoke with concern.

"I'll take him to the truck. You guys go on." I took Mac by his collar to help him walk slowly back to the truck. His legs continued to be weak and wobbly.

At the truck, Mac sprawled out on his belly in the snow, continuing to pant hard. I got him a bowl of water and set it before him. He drank it all and didn't even get up to drink it. I got him a second bowl, which he drank in the same manner. His panting had subsided. After about fifteen minutes or so, his breathing returned to normal, and he was up walking normal. What was wrong? What just happened? It was sunny but thirty-two degrees, and there was snow on the ground. I wouldn't think he would overheat or have a heat-stroke in these conditions. This was very concerning. Mac seemed fully recovered and was anxious to get out for more hunting. I wasn't going to take any chances. "I'm sorry, baby boy. I think you should rest longer. Load up!" Mac obeyed. I rolled the windows down a bit for air to get in but not enough for Mac to get out. Then, a little reluctantly, I left to join the boys.

When we got back to the truck, Mac was back to his normal self. He was happy to see us. He bounded out of the truck and was checking everything out. As we loaded up to head home, the owner came out to check how our hunt went. As he trained and bred dogs, we asked him what he thought of Mac's incident. "Well, I've seen that happen with dogs who had bad hips. Not much you can do about it." We didn't respond to that but thanked him for the birds and the hunt. Bad hips! I don't think so! We've had his hips and elbows x-rayed, and they were OFA (Orthopedic Foundation for Animals Inc.) approved. This was very concerning. We'd have to call the vet first thing Monday morning.

The vet was able to see us Monday afternoon. We walked in to the waiting area and up to the front desk. "Good morning! How can we help you today?" the receptionist greeted us, to which Mac wagged his tail and jumped up putting his front paws on the counter. The receptionist patted his head and gave him a treat. "You bad boy!" I teased and tugged Mac's collar to sit next to me. "We have an appointment for Mac Motland."

"Oh yes. Just one moment, and I'll get a room ready for you." Mac got busy exploring the room. There are all kinds of interesting smells in a veterinary clinic. He checked out the bin of kids' toys and then back around to the front counter with me in tow.

"Okay, Ms. Motland, right this way." She held open the door that separated the long hall to the examining rooms. "Let's get a weight on him first." She directed us to the scale against the wall. I led Mac to step on the scale. "Good boy! Sit." Mac sat briefly then stepped off. I led him around to the scale again. "Sit." After a few tries, he finally sat long enough for us to get a good read on his weight. "Seventy-three pounds. Okay, come this way." She led us to the room and closed the door once we were inside.

I sat down on the bench next to the examining table. Mac got busy sniffing every reachable surface. "Come here, buddy." I gave him a little tug on his leash. He came to me with a big smile and his tongue hanging out. I gave him a big hug, and he gave me a big wet kiss. "Thank you. You're the best puppy in the world." The door began to open, and Mac was right there to check it out.

"Well, hello there, Mac!" The doctor leaned over to pet Mac's head and closed the door behind her. "Hi, what are we here for today?" She reached over to shake my hand.

"Well, we had a bit of a scary incident this weekend." I proceeded to tell her the details of the event.

"Hmm. That doesn't sound good." She knelt down and took Mac's head in her hands. She then checked his eyes, teeth, and gums. "We'll just have to look at you, Mac." She took her stethoscope to check his heart and lungs. "I just love listening to a working dog's heart." She smiled at Mac, who gave her a tail wag and a big kiss.

"Well, everything looks good. His temp is normal. His heart and lungs sound good. His eyes, gums, and teeth are all good. We know his hips and elbows are good, and I don't feel any problem in his muscles. There is a genetic disease in Labradors that there is new research on. It's exercise-induced collapse, or EIC. It occurs in Labradors during exercise with high excitement. Their rear legs become wobbly, and they collapse. If they are stopped at first sign of weakness or wobbliness, they usually recover. However, some dogs have died during an episode."

"Died?" My heart sank. "Is there any treatment or medication available? How do we know for certain this is what he has?"

The doctor paused. "There isn't any treatment currently other than to watch him and avoid situations that would trigger an episode. The testing requires a tissue sample from Mac's haunches. It is very invasive and expensive."

"What do you recommend?" I asked.

"I think for now, keep an eye on him and stop at any sign of weakness or wobbliness. Have him rest for fifteen to twenty minutes before continuing. Other than that, Mac is a very healthy, happy boy." We looked at Mac smiling, and I patted his head.

"Okay then. Thank you, Doctor. We'll keep an eye on him."

"Here is some more information on EIC." She handed me a three-page article and opened the door for Mac and me.

As we headed out to the car, Mac was examining everything in his usual fashion. I was deep in thought and very troubled by this news. "Well, Mac, we're just going to keep a close eye on you. We'll just have to take breaks during our hunts and give you lots of water. Load up, puppy." Mac jumped into the front passenger seat, turned, and gave me a kiss. "You're the best boy in the whole world. Watch your nose." I waited for him to sit down again so I could close the door.

CHAPTER 9

Life Goes On

With a plan for Mac's condition, we continued as usual, and the whole situation faded. I continued to work with Mac on our hunting and handling skills with Linda. During our times together with Linda, she would explain why we were doing certain things a certain way. Gradually she was exposing me to AKC (American Kennel Club) hunt tests and how they worked. She suggested that I should sign up to run Mac in a Junior Hunt Test. I was not so sure about this idea. I felt very insecure about my knowledge and skills to perform in an AKC event, but I was happy to learn about it. Gradually, my confidence grew, and I became more open to the idea of running Mac in a hunt test. After all, if we're going to breed him, we've got to get him out in front of breeders and possibly get him awards. The first taste of such an event happened when Linda had a Fun Day, inviting clients, friends, and colleagues to a day of birds for the dogs and an opportunity for their owners to experience a hunt test without the pressure of a real hunt test.

The event was held at Greenleaf's Farm. There were ten to fifteen dogs with their owners, families, and friends. In our green diesel pickup, Mike, Mac and I drove back into the fields on a dirt road. Mac was standing up between us in the front seat, watching intently.

Dogs barked at us as we drove by those who had staked out their spot along the road and were setting up chairs with their dogs on leads next to them. We kept going up toward what appeared to be the center of activity. There were tables and canopies set up, and there was Linda, directing everyone. She saw us and came over to the truck as we slowed down. "Welcome! You'll want to find a spot just up to the left." She pointed ahead of us where the road forked to the right and the left about fifty feet ahead. "Set up in the shade and then come down here to sign in. We'll start running the dogs on the field in front of you. You'll get your number to run when you sign in."

We thanked Linda and headed up to the left as directed. It was a sunny northwest spring day. The morning mist was burning off, and we were expecting a warm afternoon. We found a spot with some shade for Mac. Mac had a beautiful thick coat. He preferred cooler temps, and when it was hot, he always managed to find water to cool off. Mud would work if water was not available. We got our chairs out and pounded Mac's tie-off in the ground, hooked Mac up, and went to sign up. The Fun Day commenced. Linda was the judge, scoring everyone's dog for each of their runs. There were two land retrieves, followed by two water retrieves. The land retrieves were first. Mac did great. He ran straight to each bird and brought them to me. When he's good, he's really good.

After all the dogs had completed the land retrieves, we took a lunch break. We all loaded up into our vehicles and moved to another area strategic to the sun's new position so we had shade for our dogs and sun for us. We all brought our chairs and circled around Linda to relax and eat the lunches we brought. Linda shared stories about AKC hunt tests and her many experiences with her Labradors. When she was done, she gathered all our dogs and went out in the field with them. They followed her as she held some bumpers and bounced around her, hoping to be the recipient of one of those bumpers. Some people have a gift with dogs. The rest of us still enjoy them but have to work harder to command the attention and respect.

After a nice break, we were ready to move the caravan over for the water retrieves. It was fun seeing all the different people and their dogs. The dogs were all Labrador retrievers and Chesapeake Bay retrievers. Some dogs did really well, and most dogs did a good job. One Chesapeake had an issue in the water. He got out about ten feet, which was about a quarter of the way to his mark, when his rear seemed to sink and he continued to work his front paws frantically but went nowhere. "Get that dog out of the water," Linda hollered as she ran over to the owner. They got him to turn around, and he was able to make it back to shore. Linda checked him over and talked with the owner. We all observed from a distance and had no idea what had happened at the time. Sometimes dogs just have a bad day. Looking back now, I think that dog had an EIC episode.

Mac did well in his water retrieves. He marked well, went straight to the bird, and brought them back over the line (Junior Hunt does not require the dog to deliver to hand). Mac was not always good at bringing back to hand, especially in the water. He always wanted to drop the bird right at the shoreline and poke at it. Today I got him past the line with the bird. Although on the second retrieve, I had to clap and run up the hill to get him to bring it past the line. We did it. It wasn't the prettiest, but we completed all the runs successfully. Everybody got a ribbon that completed all the runs. So Mac and I got our first ribbon. It was a fun day, and it got me thinking, maybe I could run Mac in a real AKC hunt test.

CHAPTER 10

Breeding—Decided

T he idea of breeding Mac was growing stronger in my mind and heart every day. To breed your dog, you need to show him, get him titles, and get out among the serious dog breeders. So here we go. I signed up for our first AKC hunt test, the Puget Sound Labrador Retriever Association's (PSLRA) spring hunt test. The hunt tests are Saturday and Sunday with three skill levels: Junior Hunter, Senior Hunter, and Master Hunter. Mac and I signed up for the juniors' stake and were to run on Sunday.

Prior to the weekend, Linda worked with Mac and me, giving us all the tips and encouragement possible with the time available. The weekend arrived. I was nervous and excited. We had received the e-mail accepting our application to run, along with the number for our turn. There were sixty-seven dogs signed up to run. We were number 7. I also received an e-mail asking if I'd like to help out on Saturday with the seniors' stake. This would be a good opportunity to see how things work before Mac and I run on Sunday. I told them yes.

On Saturday, I was up early to get to the hunt test by 8:00 a.m. It was a beautiful morning, which would help the forty-five-minute drive north go by quickly. The tests were being held at Pepper's Farm in Carnation, Washington. Since the hunt tests are to simulate hunting, you need to wear appropriate camo or dark clothing. I had on my dark-green jeans with a camo t-shirt and camo coat. Layering is necessary for spring in the northwest. You layer up for the cooler mornings and then strip down to your t-shirt by lunchtime.

My first assignment was manning a bird station for the water run. There were two stations for this run, two marks. One with live birds and my station had dead birds. When given the signal by the judge, we were to quack the duck call, fire the starter pistol, release the duck from the launcher, then reload the launcher with a new duck to be ready for the next dog. I had a young man helping me. He was around thirteen years old. His parents were involved in the hunt tests, and you could tell he'd done this once or twice. He was relaxed and easy to talk with, which helped pass the time as we waited for the dog to complete his second retrieve. At one point, I was admiring a duck I was preparing to put in the launcher. It was a mallard drake—a green head, as we hunters call them. His feathers glistened as I folded his wings in and placed him carefully in the launcher. "Sorry, little guy. It's for a good cause."

"Ah, it's just a dumb bird," the young man retorted.

"Well, maybe. But he's still a beautiful creation of God and deserves respect as all life does." We were both quieter after that exchange. Hopefully, he was thinking about the value of that duck and life.

Once the final dog had gone, there was a short break for lunch, and then on to the next station. This was a water/land run for the dog. I was to place a bird in a clump of grass just up from the water. The judge showed me how to lay the bird so some of it was visible but most of it was not. My part was just a third of the station. There were two other marks that other people were manning. I was placing the bird for the blind retrieve where the handler directs their dog to the bird using whistles and hand gestures. At one point, I was running out of birds and had to flag the judge for more birds. Guess who delivered my bag of birds? Chuck Hilton, Mac's breeder. He and Sharon were very involved in the PSLRA and also judged in AKC hunt tests. "Hi, Chuck!" I beamed at him.

He smiled and said hi, but I don't think he remembered me.

Perfect, I thought. *An opportunity to be in front of Chuck that I hadn't expected. Maybe he'll see Mac run tomorrow.* As it turned out, it was probably a good thing that Chuck was involved in other aspects of the hunt test and did not see our run.

We weren't as lucky for the weather on Sunday as Saturday. It was a more typical northwest spring day, overcast and light rain. Mike and I got up early; put together some snacks; loaded up Mac and all his gear; loaded up our rain gear, chairs, and umbrellas; and headed off to Pepper's Farm. We were going to meet Linda there. She would be my moral support, give me tips, help with Mac, etc. We got there early to check in and find out where to park and set up. At ten minutes to 8:00 a.m., Linda had not arrived yet. I began to get nervous. At eight o'clock, all the handlers running dogs for the junior test gathered around the judge to listen to the setup. There would be two marks. The first took the dog through water to retrieve the bird on land. The handler would hold the dog's collar and release the dog on the judge's cue. The second mark was a land retrieve. The first retrieve would have a live bird; the second, a previously shot bird.

We returned to our vehicles and dogs to wait for our turn. As I headed back to the truck, there was Linda talking to Mike. I relaxed a bit. Being number 7 didn't give us a whole lot of time. Linda checked over Mac's collar and let him out of the truck on his leash. All dogs are to be in control at AKC events, meaning they're on their leash until their turn. There are three blinds (basically a camouflage screen) set up about ten feet apart leading to the starting point of the run. As the first dog is running, dogs 2, 3, and 4 are waiting for their turn behind each blind. This is so the dog does not see the other dogs running. That would be cheating. Being number 7 meant we were up to the first blind in about thirty minutes.

Mac loves hunting, and he got very excited hearing the gunshots. It took all my strength to keep him from looking around the blind. He would not sit still, and my nervousness was not helping either one of us. When I got him to lie down, he would try to get his nose underneath the blind to peek out. We finally made it to the last blind without him cheating. I held his leash short, keeping Mac close to me, and watched the dog ahead of us looking over the blind. The dog did well. He got both the birds and brought them to the handler's hand. This is where Mac was not the best. He was great at the mark, bringing the bird back almost to you, and then he wanted to inspect the bird. Luckily, this is a Junior Hunt Test. We only had to get him to cross the line with the bird. "I know you can do this, Mac. We got this." I patted Mac's head. He ignored me and was focused on what was beyond the blind.

The dog finished his run, and the judges flagged for us to proceed to the line. "Mac, heel!" We got up to the line. As calmly as possible, I slipped my finger in Mac's collar and released his leash, dropping it behind me. I waved behind my back to the judges that we were ready. They flagged the station to go. *Quack, quack, quack!* Mac was focused on where the quacking came from but was steady. The bird was released, and *bang!* The bird dropped. Mac was pulling slightly. I released his collar and commanded, "Mac!" He ran out, jumped into the water, and swam straight across the water onto the land, and got the bird. *Toot, toot, toot!* "Here, Mac!" He came right back in the same line through the water, stopped right at the edge, dropped the bird, and began investigating it. "Mac, here! Fetch it here!" I stepped toward him and didn't realize that I crossed the line. This eliminated us. If I had instead backed up, he would have picked up the bird to follow me just like we had done on Linda's Fun Day. Argh!

"Sorry, that's a fail. You can go ahead and run your dog on the landmark though." So Mac and I lined up for the land bird. *Quack, quack, quack!* The bird was released with the launcher, and *bang!* I released Mac. He ran straight to it, gave it a glance, and ran past it, beginning to hunt. I gave him the "sit" whistle and tried to bring him back to the bird. He sat and followed my directives but just didn't believe I could want that cold, slimy, dead bird. Mac had only worked with live birds. I tried for a minute or so. Then the judges flagged the helpers to pick the bird up. I brought Mac in; we thanked the judges and headed back to the truck, where Mike and Linda were waiting for us. Linda came out to Mac, bended over, and grabbed his face. "Aww, you didn't like that cold, slimy bird? Well, I don't blame you." She took his leash and loaded him up into the truck.

Mike came over and gave me a big hug. "Well, we know our boy can do it. Next time." I wasn't feeling very confident at that moment—not so much about Mac, but about my ability as a handler. It was starting to rain harder, so we decided to head home rather than watch the other dogs.

CHAPTER 11

The Next Step

I continued to work with Linda once a week. The more I worked with Mac, the more I wanted to breed him. I've been told by many people what a beautiful dog he is and that he has such a sweet nature. How fun it would be to have one of his puppies. We'd have to get *cheese* in the puppy's name somehow, so we'd have Mac and Cheese. Maybe Chez would work? I finally got enough nerve to call Chuck and Sharon about breeding Mac. We needed them to give the okay and to change his registration, which currently limited him from being bred. I got right to the point. "I want to breed Mac. What do we need to do?"

There was a pause. "Well, I guess we could talk about showing him and see how that goes."

"Okay. Where do we start?" We then set up to meet with Chuck and Sharon the following Saturday to discuss all that would be involved.

It was still northwest spring weather, misty and overcast. Mac, Mike, and I loaded up in the truck to drive north to Chuck and Sharon's. Memories of the first drive up this way filled my mind, first meeting Mac at four weeks old, not ready to leave Mom yet. He was so cute and cuddly. Then coming up to finally bring him home at nine weeks old. Mac was now three years old. A lot of time and experiences had passed since then. I pulled out of my thoughts as we passed through the town of Machias. We were almost there. I began to feel nervous and excited.

Sharon and Chuck came out to greet us as we pulled into their driveway. We climbed out and exchanged hugs. Then we let Mac out, who greeted them with tail wags and did his best to find a way to give them kisses every time they bent down to pet him. "I used to bend down to give the dogs hugs." Sharon laughed. "But I learned after a sore lip or two that that's not such a good idea." She bent to pat Mac but kept her face away from his kisses. "Well, let's go in to discuss things." Chuck turned toward the house. Mike put Mac back in the truck, and we followed Chuck and Sharon into their house. Chuck took our coats and hung them on hooks with Labradors in the entry then led us into the dining room. "Can we get you water or coffee?" Sharon asked.

"I think we're good. Thank you!" Mike replied.

Once again, we were sitting around their dining room table. This time, I was nervous but anxious to hear what their thoughts are. Chuck got right to the point. "If it's all right with you, I'd like to start by getting Mac his Junior Hunter title. I'm confident I can get him his title by the end of summer. After that, we'll move on to showing him." He waited for our response.

Mike and I looked at each other. "That would be great," I replied. I felt relieved too. Although I enjoy running Mac, Chuck is far more experienced and can get Mac his title quicker.

"I've listed dates of hunt tests I'd like to run him and the expense involved. Entry fees, motel, and fuel come to about $715." Chuck showed the list to Mike and me, and we looked over the dates and numbers. Our chairs creaked as we leaned forward on the table to look over the list.

"You would certainly be able to achieve this faster than I would. The sooner the better, right?" I looked at Mike then Chuck and Sharon.

Mike looked at the list again. "The costs look reasonable. The hunt tests are all in July. Will you keep Mac the whole time?" Mike asked. I swallowed as I looked at Chuck for his answer.

"Yes, he'll need to stay with me that month and a few weeks prior for training."

I hadn't considered that. I knew Mac would be in good hands, but to be without my fur baby a whole month … I looked at Mike. He looked at me and quietly affirmed, "We need to do this if we want to go forward."

We discussed a few more details, and Chuck gave me the entries for the four hunt tests with some notes on how to fill them out. We shook hands, gathered our papers, and returned to the truck where Mac awaited us, clueless of our plans and schemes for him. We would return Mac with his food and bedding in a couple of weeks. Mac would then begin his adventure with Chuck.

Those two weeks went by quickly. Before I was ready, the agreed date to take Mac to the Hiltons arrived. I tried to be happy and excited for Mac. I didn't want to project any negative emotion to him. "You are going to love this, Mac. You are going to get so many birds you'll be in heaven," I told Mac as I loaded his food and bedding in the car. "Load up, Mac!" We were off, me and Mac, to the Hiltons.

CHAPTER 12

Junior Hunter

Just prior to Mac's hunt-test adventure, we had a family gathering at the home of Mike's mom. She had an indoor pool. Mike's daughter, son-in-law, four grandkids, Mike, Mac, and I had a fun day of visiting and playing in the pool. I took several pictures of Mac jumping into the pool after the balls the kids threw for him. I taped these pictures around my computer screen, hoping it would help me not miss him so much. All the hunt tests were several hours away. Because of this, the plan was for us to not come to the first two but come to the last two. These were the last weekend of July at Sauvie Island Wildlife Area in Oregon. These would also be the last hunt tests. We would come watch Mac and then bring him home with us.

Chuck kept us posted via e-mail on Mac's progress. "Well, Mac got his first stake just barely." Chuck liked to tease me that Mac was spoiled. "He needs more structure," he'd tell me. Structure? We get up at the same time most days, we take our walk, he goes to work with me, we walk at lunch—what more do you want?

You're the trainer. Fix him, I'd think. It took me a while to stop being defensive and realize he just liked to tease me.

The last weekend of July finally arrived. We were to meet Chuck (and Mac) at the hunt test on Saturday by 8:00 a.m. The tests began at 8:30 a.m. Mac had passed both of his prior stakes. Now he had to pass both stakes this weekend to get his official AKC Junior Hunter title. It was incredibly hot that weekend in Oregon. Okay, for us northwesterners, ninety degrees is incredibly hot. Mac, with his beautiful thick coat, was not a real hot-weather guy either.

We arrived at 8:00 a.m. as planned and looked for Chuck and his truck. Following the signs for the Junior Hunt Tests, we were able to find him fairly quickly. He had his truck set up in the shade. Mac was in a wire kennel in the back of his truck. "Hi, buddy. Such a good boy! I've missed you so much." Mac smiled at me.

"Hey, don't mess with him. He's got work to do. You can fuss with him later." Chuck smiled and motioned for us to sit down with him in the shade. We discussed Chuck's thoughts on Mac's possibilities for achieving his title this weekend. "He's got a pretty good chance. There are often circumstances that happen, or a judge doesn't like the dog, or the dog can just be having a bad day. We'll just do our best."

The first run was a land retrieve. The handler and the dog start on a slight mound. The bird is released and downed into some thick cover. To make the retrieve, the dog must run down the mound, past a little pool of refreshing water, up a slight mound to find the bird in the cover, then back straight to the handler past that refreshing pool of water. This was considered a difficult run for the junior level. I was nervous—not because of the difficulty. I knew Mac could do that retrieve, no problem. It was the water. If he detours to the water, he'll get marked down.

Many dogs ran before Mac. A fair number of them had difficulty and were not able to make the retrieve. They had to mark it well and then hunt the bird up in the thick cover. Mac and Chuck were making their way through the blinds for their turn. "I'm so nervous." I grabbed Mike's arm.

"Mac has passed two tests now, and Chuck has run many dogs through many tests," Mike replied softly to me.

"Yeah, it's just that water."

"I know. I'm nervous too," Mike confessed.

Chuck was flagged to come up to the line with Mac. Chuck signaled that he is ready. The judge flagged for the bird to be released. *Quack, quack, quack! Bang!* Chuck released Mac. He headed straight for the bird. He had marked it well. Because of the thick cover, he had to hunt for the bird. He stayed on it and got the bird. Mike and I looked at each other. One hurdle accomplished. *Toot, toot, toot!* "Here, Mac!" Chuck called Mac. Mac was heading straight to Chuck when he caught that refreshing pool of water in his peripheral. Yup, he detoured. But he kept the bird in his mouth and returned after a quick dip. Not good. We wouldn't know how much that will affect his score until the end of the day. For now, we met up with Chuck and Mac at the truck and waited for the next run.

Back at the truck, Chuck had given Mac water and had placed him in the wire crate already. "Are you a happy boy?" I cooed at Mac. He loves hunting and getting birds. And he's wet. He couldn't be happier. Chuck left the back of the truck open and had a tarp set up to one side to provide shade for Mac as the sun moved across the sky. "Hey, Chuck! What do you think? Did he make it?" I cheerfully greeted Chuck.

"Well, it wasn't pretty, but I think just barely," Chuck grunted.

"That's my boy." I smiled. He always gets the job done and loves every minute. We sat in the shade, passing the time in conversation, waiting for the next run.

The next run was a water retrieve. Mac loves to retrieve in water. He always does a big jump into the water with all he's got. However, if he can save time by running on land, shortening the swim, he does it. They call that squaring the retrieve. In some books, they would call this being a smart dog. However, for AKC hunt tests, they are to swim straight to the mark from the handler and straight back in the same line. In the junior stake, however, as long as he swims to the mark, he can run the bird back on land.

Mac and Chuck were up to run. Chuck signaled to the judge that he's ready. The judge flagged the helpers. *Quack, quack, quack! Bang!* Chuck released Mac. "Oh no! He's running the land!" Mike whispered to me. Not too far though, and he jumped in the water. He got the bird and headed to shore running the land back to Chuck. "Not perfect. We'll have to wait and see what happens." Mike and I rolled our eyes at each other and headed back to the truck to meet Chuck and Mac. We walked up as Chuck was finishing giving Mac his water.

"Load up, boy." Mac happily complied. He's had a great day of birds and water. He's the happiest boy ever. Chuck turned and gave us a wry grin. "Well, I think he did it, but just barely!"

I turned to Mac. "You're the best, Mac. Such a good boy!"

Chuck rolled his eyes at me and turned to sit down in his camp chair. "Now it's more waiting."

Mac passed all his stakes that weekend, getting the four ribbons needed for his AKC Junior Hunter title. We gave our goodbyes and thanks to Chuck then loaded Mac up with us to head home. Mac lay on my lap in the front seat and gave a big sigh. "Now you're back with us full-time, baby boy. We missed you so much!" I rubbed his head and ears as he snuggled deeper into my lap.

Mike reached over to rub Mac's head. "Nice to have you back buddy."

CHAPTER 13

Back to the Routine

We all slipped back into the daily routines of walks, training, and work (Mike and I). Working with Mac on his drills and exercise had Mike and me thinking about having more acreage. We built our current home, and it was perfect for us, except the yard. The lot was not ideal for a larger dog. It was on a hill that we terraced, and it was beautiful but only afforded a small area of grass. It was located on a quiet cul-de-sac just off a very busy street with traffic lights. One day, the UPS delivered a package to our house. Mac and I greeted the driver, who gave Mac a dog biscuit. I turned to go in the house thinking Mac was right behind me as the driver drove off. As I put the package inside the house, I realized Mac was not right behind me. I took off running down the street, calling Mac. As I got to the busy intersection, I saw Mac on the other side of the street. He had chased the UPS truck across the busy intersection. I quickly gave him the "sit" whistle, which he responded to, thankfully. Then when it was safe, I crossed the street and took hold of his collar. I was so thankful that he was okay.

Visions of acreage were now on our minds. We love the outdoors, and now with Mac, it was a necessity. We began actively looking with a real estate agent for a home on five acres, minimum. The house was not totally necessary as we could live in our travel trailer until we could build. But then having a house would be nice. Our agent faithfully sent us listings weekly. Two or more weekends each month for three years, we would go out with her to look at the properties we were interested in. A lot of them were overpriced. Some were on a hill, and the acreage was unusable. In others, the house was way too big or was in disrepair. We finally found a property that had great potential. It was twenty-four acres with a mobile home and a four-bay garage with a carriage house on a lake. It had one thousand feet on Fish Lake on one side of the property and a pond on the other.

"I love it," I told Mike. "This is a perfect place for Mac." We climbed back in the truck where Mac was waiting for us. He gave us a tail wag and kissed Mike on the side of his face.

"I don't know. There's a lot of junk, and we can't see the inside of the buildings yet," Mike hesitantly replied.

"Well, let's talk to our realtor more before we decide." We called her as we headed out of the driveway to set up a time to meet.

Prior to our scheduled meeting, our realtor called to inform us that the owners had accepted an offer on the property that was below the asking price and was contingent on the buyer selling their home. I was so disappointed. The one we actually felt excited about and wanted to make an offer was sold. I was expressing this disappointment to my sister-in-law that night at their home. "A day late and a dollar short," I moaned to Donna.

"Why don't you make a counteroffer?" Donna tossed out as she pulled the salad dressing out of the fridge.

"What? We can do that?"

"Yes. Make an offer for the full amount with no contingency." Donna poured the dressing on the salad and began tossing it.

"I didn't know that. I like it." I became excited as hope rose up in my heart.

The next morning, we called our realtor, and she sent the offer to the owners. The housing market was good in our area, and we felt confident our home would sell quickly. Meanwhile, Mike's mom agreed to cover the down payment until our home sold. The following day, we got the news. Our offer was accepted! There was paper-work to be signed the following week, and everything was to close by the end of the month. At this point, we still hadn't seen the inside of the buildings. The renters were to vacate prior to closing, and we could inspect the buildings then. This was a bit of a risk, but the property was worth it, and Mike could build and fix anything!

We met with our realtor when the renters had vacated. There was junk everywhere: an empty trailer with cats, a plastic child's play set at one corner of the property, and broken plywood at one spot that looked like maybe it was a jump for a bike. The garage / carriage house was a mess, but we knew what to do with that. The one bed-room was upstairs, and there was no closet. The one bathroom was at the bottom of the stairs from the bedroom with one sink and was small. From there, you come to the kitchen with room for the fridge, one counter, and space for a table. The living room was next to the kitchen with one entry door and a couple of windows. A cement board was in the corner where a woodstove had once sat. The hole for the chimney was patched but not very well. There was a white ceil-ing fan that had a modest pad attached to it, for balance we guessed. Another door off the kitchen went into a garage that was half the size of the three garage bays next to it. There was a washer and dryer in the garage, but they did not work.

The three large garage bays were separate and had been rented to people for storage. Nothing had been cleaned in some time, but the structure was sound. We knew we could deal with cleaning and making the place into our cozy home. The mobile home was another matter. It was newer but had been trashed by the renters. There was no flooring anywhere, just bare plywood. The kitchen counters were chipped, and much of the laminate had been torn up. The one bath-room had a broken, unusable toilet, and the shower base was dam-aged and would need to be replaced. Being just a mobile home, this was not worth the work, time, or money to make it livable.

The carriage house passed all the inspections. Our inspector was very excited about the property and the existing well. So the final requirements were for the seller to remove the trailer with cats and the other items left around the property by the renters and to remove and dispose of the mobile home. They weren't happy about the mobile-home removal but complied. The sale closed in January, and we began our adventure to make our carriage house livable and to sell our home.

By June, our carriage house was ready for us to move in, and our previous home would close by June 15. On June 27, we moved in to our cozy new home. We moved from a three-bedroom home with master bath, walk-in closet, and two additional bathrooms to a one-bedroom, one-bathroom house. The garage off the kitchen was now a pantry / laundry room and office. We added windows in the living room, moved the door, installed a new woodstove and a new ceiling fan. The kitchen got new cabinets, countertops, sink, and the space for a table was filled with cabinets and a stove/oven. The three garage bays were connected with openings, and the first bay had an enclosed room in the back for hunting gear, my piano, and exercise equipment.

One afternoon, as I was walking around the property with Mike's mom, Grace, she asked, "So what are you going to call this place?"

Call it? I thought. "I guess I hadn't considered naming it," I replied. "It's the perfect place for Mac. There's the trails and water on both sides of the property. He's in heaven here."

"So then, how about MacHaven?" she asked.

"Yeah. I like that. MacHaven it is."

CHAPTER 14

Back in Pursuit

Once we settled into our new home, training Mac and the pursuit for titles for recognition and breeding resumed. We kept in contact with Chuck and Sharon, asking their opinions about things that came up with Mac. Chuck took us to his spot for waterfowl hunting twice, which was pretty special. But progress on getting Mac more titles to show him for breeding seemed to stop. It seemed like the conversation was avoided, and I began to give up on the idea. Mike had expressed that having two hunting dogs would perhaps help us be more successful in upland hunting. So I considered getting another puppy not from Mac. Mac was five and a half years old now. I didn't want to wait too long to get a puppy. I wanted Mac to be young enough to play with and put up with a puppy. So I began searching breeders for any who were expecting puppies.

I had met another couple involved in hunt tests who bred and judged just like the Hiltons. I checked their website and found they were expecting a litter. I expressed interest for a puppy on her website. She was very excited and called me within an hour. "You are the perfect people for our puppies. We want people who will run our dogs in hunt tests. We will work with you to train the puppy. When can you meet with us?" I was taken back a little at first. I didn't expect such an exuberant response. After I got my bearings, we set up to meet with them the following week. We knew their dam and had seen her at AKC events. She had the same sire as Mac. That was a plus. They showed us pictures of the sire of the upcoming puppies. He was chosen for his beautiful thick coat. Mike nudged me and whispered, "His legs are short."

The breeder overheard and retorted, "He is an AKC Labrador and will add to the dam's traits." Mike refrained from further comment, and we talked more about training and hunt tests. "We will let you know when the puppies arrive. Once we know how many and that there is a yellow for you, we'll expect a deposit to hold your puppy."

We shook hands and exchanged pleasantries. We then piled in the truck, where Mac awaited, and we headed home. "I did not like the look of that sire." Mike was adamant. "I don't want a dog that looks like him. The dam is beautiful. But the sire ..." Mike shook his head.

"Yeah, I know. Let's just wait and find out if she's really pregnant." I tried to stall the inevitable no forming in Mike.

While we waited for news about the puppies, Chuck called. "I've heard you're thinking about getting a puppy?"

Wait, I think, *I don't remember mentioning this to either Chuck or Sharon.* The dog world is a small world.

Chuck continued, "There's a pup from Ranger who needs to be rehomed. She's about ten months old and was being trained to be a service dog. They think her prey instincts are too strong. I think she'd be a great dog for you guys." Ranger was working on his Master Hunter title when Mac was working on his Junior Hunter title. He's a beautiful dog, and we liked his looks. We love him and his owner/handler. Mike, overhearing the call, began grinning. I could tell Short Legs was out and a Ranger pup was more to his liking.

"Well, okay. I think we're interested," I haltingly told him.

"Great! Here is the breeder's name and phone number." I wrote it down. "I'll call her and let her know you're interested."

There were many details to work out between the company who had the dog and the two owners of the sire and the dam. The dog was in another state and would have to be flown here. After many calls and funds being exchanged, the date was set for her arrival at the airport. Meanwhile, we needed a name. They had named her Wrigley, after a ballpark. It just didn't ring our bells. So we began throwing different names back and forth. We landed on Molly for her call name. Now for the registered name. For at least a week, we were throwing out different thoughts throughout our time together. "How about By Golly Ms. Molly?" Mike scrunched up his face.

"Not bad, but that's just not it."

The breeder then suggested Unsinkable Molly Brown. "After all, she's been through a lot in her first ten months. She's not giving up."

Mike and I thought about it for a week, and it grew on us. She would be registered as Glen Eden's Unsinkable Molly Brown. Molly would be arriving soon. We were very excited.

CHAPTER 15

The Next Adventure

Molly was to arrive in the afternoon at SeaTac Airport. The breeder would go in to sign papers and get Molly. Mike and I were to meet her in the parking lot where Molly would arrive. "We have a surprise for you, Mac! You are getting a playmate." I loaded Mac in the car, and off we went to the airport. As we pulled into the parking lot, the breeder already had Molly out and was letting her stretch and potty in the parking lot. "There she is, Mac! Oh, she's beautiful. I hope you like her." Mac was just happy to be going for a ride. We found a parking spot and opened the door to get out. Mac was close behind, pushing his nose out the opening. "You wait, Mac. Watch your nose." Mac backed up, and I shut the door.

Molly was exploring every bush in her path, oblivious to the fact that she had just flown many miles to have a new life with the Motland pack. "Hi, Cheri! Nice to finally meet you in person." I reached out to shake her hand.

"Yes, nice to meet you too, Mike." She shook Mike's hand. "Well, they said she was real skitterish, but I don't see it. She seems calm and confident to me," Cheri observed as Molly finally found the spot for business.

"Yes, she seems very calm. Let's see how she does with Mac." We walked over to the car where Mac waited leaving noseprints on every window as he tried to watch our every move. I opened the back of the car, and Molly went right over to check Mac out. He responded in like kind. I put Mac's leash on so he can get out and they can sniff each other on the same level.

"Friends already. That's great! I'll check in on you to see how they're getting along. Feel free to call anytime." Cheri shook our hands again.

"Thanks so much, Cheri. We are very excited about Molly. We'll keep you posted." I turned to the dogs. "Load up, pups!" Mac jumped in and Molly followed. Off we went on our hour drive to MacHaven, Molly's new home.

Molly was yellow, like Mac, but had a smaller frame. Being just eleven months now (the whole process of getting her took a month), she would probably fill out a little bit more. She was more delicate and looked more feminine than Mac. As we would soon see, she loved to hunt as much as Mac. I began working with Molly along with Mac on our morning walks. Molly had received good basic obedience training; now she needed to learn hunting skills. Working with two dogs was a whole new dynamic for me, especially when they were so different. Mac was sure of himself and calm. Molly was not as confident but really wants to please. She wanted to please so badly she would run in a circle when she didn't understand what you wanted. My confidence in my ability to train didn't help the situation either. I would get frustrated easily, and that would cause Molly to do more circles. I probably needed to give both of them one-on-one time but didn't feel like I had that time. So every morning, I'd pray for patience and for God to help me be the trainer my dogs needed me to be.

Molly arrived in April, and in May, she would become one year old on the twenty-eighth. About two weeks before Molly's birthday, we noticed some blood drops on the floor. After checking both dogs carefully and checking their paws and nails, we realized what it was: Molly was in heat. We didn't plan this one ahead of time. It caught us by surprise. I had to make a quick run to the pet store to buy some diapers for Molly. We also hadn't worked through or given any thought to how we would handle this. Our breeders keep their

females in heat in separate buildings from the males to avoid accidental breedings. Mac and Molly are family members. How are we going
to keep them separate? We decided we would keep an eye on them
and never leave them together when we weren't there.

This seemed to work for a while. Mac didn't seem to even notice
until about a week into it. Then Molly was prancing up to him, flag-
ging him. His eyes were big, and he would try to mount her. We
would intervene and redirect their attention. The morning of Molly's
birthday, I walked Mike to the door as he was leaving for work. We
said our usual goodbyes with hugs and kisses, and I waved as he
drove down the driveway. I turned to go back to the kitchen, and
I saw Mac and Molly. They were connected but turned away from
each other, both panting, and their eyes were looking away. *Oh no!
This is not good. It just didn't look right. That's got to be hurting Mac*, I
thought. I tried to separate them but was concerned I'd hurt them. I
was lacking in my knowledge of how this worked with dogs and only
could relate to humans. It just looked like it was hurting Mac. So I
called the emergency vet. It was too early for our normal vet.

The receptionist answered. I paused, wondering how I would
communicate this to her. So I just blurted it out rather excitedly,
"My two dogs are stuck together, and they're panting strongly. I can't
separate them, and it looks like it really hurts. I mean, they're sitting
butt to butt. It just doesn't look right." I must have made that receptionist's day.

She responded very professionally, and I didn't hear the slightest
giggle. "They'll be fine. Just leave them alone for a bit, and they'll
return to normal."

"Oh. Okay. Thank you." I hung up. I looked over at Mac and
Molly. "Well, you two. We really didn't want this so early, but I guess
we're having puppies."

CHAPTER 16

Puppies!

A nother book now was added to our library on dogs, *Breeding Dogs for Dummies.* Canine pregnancy lasts approximately fifty-nine to sixty-three days. Within the first three weeks, the fetus is formed. At forty-three days, an x-ray can be taken. Many breeders do this to see how many puppies there are. Now we wait and watch to see if Molly is really pregnant. Dogs can have false pregnancies. Meanwhile, we need to inform our breeders. We'll be looking to them for guidance through this whole process. Chuck and Sharon were very kind about the accidental breeding and were willing to offer their knowledge and experience. Most of this would be obtained by e-mail and phone as our move to MacHaven increased our distance apart.

I began reading the book on breeding dogs. I skipped through the first sections of the book and went right to the section on prenatal care, whelping, and raising the puppies. I'd have to catch up on the rest later. Besides collecting some items to have on hand such as clean rags (to aid in cleaning after birth of the puppies), disposable latex gloves, cotton thread (to use if needed to tie off the umbilical cord), different-colored ribbon (to identify the puppies), infrared lamp (to keep the puppies warm), there's the whelping box. My wonderful husband is a general contractor with an abundance of carpentry skills. I come up with the ideas, and he does them! He's amazing. Some of my ideas have been a waterfall and pond we put in at our first home, planters at the top of our stairway and above the entry, and lighting under the planter above the entry. Oh yes, and the dog bed with nightstand that allows one of the dogs to sleep next to our bed. Now he gets to make a whelping box.

The whelping box was not my idea. We put together ideas from the book and those we'd seen while researching the cost to purchase one. They were too expensive for our budget, and Mike was ready to take on the challenge to build one. The whelping box would be for Molly to have her puppies in and then to house the puppies. The box had to be big enough for Molly to lie on her side fully stretched out. One side needed to be low enough to allow easy access for Molly. We also wanted a pig rail around the interior. This is a shelf around the wall that gives the pups a crawl space to escape if needed when Molly stretches out. We set up the whelping box in our office. We didn't have a place outside or in the garage that made sense, and all other rooms in the house were too small. Now we needed to let Molly get acquainted with it and comfortable with it.

The daily walks and training for Mac and Molly continued as normal. The vet said there wasn't any need to change anything for Molly. She'll let you know if she's uncomfortable with anything. For now, more waiting and watching. At forty-three days, we made an appointment with the vet to x-ray Molly's tummy. We were so excited to know how many puppies to expect. Molly's teats were swollen, but there were no other visible signs that she was pregnant. The vet technicians led Molly to the back for the x-ray. I sat, alone, in the exam room, waiting. Finally, the vet tech brought Molly back to the exam room. "The doctor will be with you in a few minutes."

"Thank you." I took Molly's leash. "Are you a good girl, missy?" Molly wagged her tail, which caused her whole body to wag with it. I call it the full-body tail wag.

The doorknob clicked, and Molly barked. "Oh, it's just me, Molly, and we have your puppies!" The vet walked in and clipped the x-ray on the white light board. I stood up to see how many puppies were in Molly's tummy. "Well, it looks like there will be eight puppies. There might be a ninth hiding back here." She pointed to a dark spot behind one of the puppies. "But that's not definite. I'd expect eight. Congratulations!"

"Thank you. We'll keep you posted." We shook hands, and the vet held the door open for Molly and me. *That's a good number*, I thought. Not too many, but just right.

May 28, Molly's birthday, was the day Mac and Molly hooked up. On July 26, fifty-nine days later, we were keeping an eye on Molly as this was the first possible day for it to happen. It was a beautiful sunny day, not too hot. Mac and Molly were outside with us as we did yard work. Molly started acting a bit uneasy, pacing some. She kept trying to get under the chaise lounge. She'd circle and scratch at the grass. "Honey!" I shouted to Mike. "Molly's acting funny."

Mike stopped clipping the blackberries and looked over at me and Molly. "Do you think it's now?"

I looked down at Molly, who continued to scratch and circle. "Maybe, she's definitely trying to nest." We'd been counting the days since Mac and Molly hooked up. It was on the early side, but within the possible range.

"I'll go call Rachel." Mike hurried inside to call his daughter, Rachel. She was hoping to bring her kids over to watch the event. Meanwhile, I tried to coax Molly to come inside to her whelping box. She was reluctant but relented after my continual urging. Then she wasn't certain about that box. She stepped in but then went to the hall and lay down on the carpet. Mike and I fussed around her, not certain what to do. Mike suggested she might prefer her crate. He hurried out to the garage to retrieve it. "Maybe she'll be more comfortable in here." He set it next to her, and she went in. Just as she stepped in, here came the first puppy. "It's a girl!"

I went to get the rags we purchased to help clean the puppies. Molly had already started cleaning her. "What a good mom, Molly. Good girl." The puppy was alive but needed mom's milk, but Molly was still not lactating. I rushed out to the kitchen where the feeding bottles were. They were still in the package, so I quickly tore the packaging off. I opened the can of formula and poured it into the bottle. I put the nipple on and shook it upside down. No fluid came out. *What?*

Mike, who was holding the first puppy close to Molly's teats in case the milk comes, hollered, "Are you coming? There still isn't any milk coming from Molly."

"There's no hole in the nipple. I have to puncture it somehow." I fumbled through kitchen drawers, trying to figure out how I was going to put a hole in it. I couldn't believe there wasn't a hole in it.

"Hey, it's okay! She's got milk! The puppy's feeding!" Mike hollered to me. Thank God! I threw the bottle and nipple in the sink. I returned to Mike and Molly just as puppy number 2 arrived. It's a boy! We helped Molly clean the puppy and let him feed before we took both of the puppies to weigh them and tie a colored ribbon on them, a different color to identify who's who, and then log the time of birth, weight, and their ribbon color. We put them in a separate container to keep them warm and out of harm's way as Molly continued birthing. After the second puppy was born, we got her over and into the whelping box. She settled in and gave birth to the rest of the puppies there. It took almost five hours for all to arrive. The grandkids arrived in that time and saw the last puppies born. They were busy running in and out of the room, holding puppies, then running outside to play. Mac came in at one point and sat by the whelping box. He looked on for a bit, wondering what all the fuss was about, then went out to the living room and lay down.

Miss Red was born at 1:53 p.m. It was over an hour and a half before the second puppy, Mr. Green, was born at 2:35 p.m. Then came Miss Pink at 2:49 p.m. and Mr. Yellow at 3:08 p.m. It was almost another hour before Mr. Lime Green showed up at 3:52 p.m. Then came Mr. Blue at 4:34 p.m. and Mr. White at 5:01 p.m. Almost an hour later, Miss Hot Pink showed up at 5:53 p.m. Eight puppies. Some had shared their stories with us about eleven or twelve puppies. I can't imagine having any more than eight. It was the perfect number.

Mac viewing birthing.

CHAPTER 17

Raising Puppies

Most of the work at this point was Molly's. We just needed to let Molly come and go as she desires to feed her puppies and watch to make sure everyone gets a chance to eat and that Molly doesn't roll on top of anyone. Molly was a good mom, very attentive and diligent to feed and clean her puppies. Every morning, I weighed each puppy on a postage scale. If it seemed one wasn't gaining like everybody else, I'd help them get a spot next feeding session. I also slept next to Molly and the puppies at night to make sure no one got stuck under their mom or any other mishap.

I was very thankful to be working part-time from home during this period. It allowed me to care for the puppies and keep a watchful eye on Molly. It was a beautiful summer and rather hot for the northwest. I had read and the breeders had shared that the puppies must not get chilled. Even a small draft could chill them, and they could die. So we had a heat lamp above the puppies. After the third night sleeping next to Molly and the pups in my shorts and tank top on top of the sleeping bag, I thought, *Surely the puppies do not need this heat lamp.* But since I was new to this and I didn't want to lose any of these puppies, I waited until I could call the vet the next morning.

"You are correct, Mrs. Motland. They should not need the heat lamp. They'll be fine."

"Great! Thank you. It's been so hot!" Perhaps another chuckle provided to the ever professional and caring vets.

I loved fussing over the puppies. Molly was good about me fussing too. She didn't mind my help. I especially loved watching them when Molly came to feed them. They made the cutest little grunt with each move they made as they worked their way to the milk bar (Molly). It was so adorable. I took pictures daily and e-mailed them to friends and family. We all had fun watching them grow. It was especially fun after their eyes opened. After twelve days, their eyes were open. Then they were climbing and trying to get out of the whelping box. A good whelping box, as Mike had made, needs to be expandable. At this point, that meant putting higher barriers up so the puppies couldn't escape. This also meant watching Molly and moving one side to let her in when she wanted. The puppies were now getting food in addition to the milk bar. This was dry puppy food blended with water to make mush, which they got twice a day. This was a messy event as the pups threw themselves into their meal, literally, which then required everyone to be wiped down and the covers in the whelping box to be changed. It was a lot of work, but I loved every minute of it.

At three weeks, these little guys were starting to need more room. Once again, the whelping box needed to expand. This time, the operation was moved to our bonus room off our garage, which currently was an exercise, piano, and hunting-gear room. Everything got moved out to the parameter, and the whelping box became part of a larger box in the center of the room, providing a pen for the pups to play, sleep, and eat. We built a fence of lattice about three feet high to contain the pups and keep them safe and away from anything we didn't want chewed. Half the box was bedding, and the other half contained wood pellets for the pups to relieve themselves. After they ate and several other times a day, I would clean out their pen. Molly could still visit the puppies regularly although they were eating more puppy food and visiting the milk bar less.

After one cleaning visit, I got distracted and forgot to take the bag of tissue I used to gather all the puppies' excrement out of their pen. I had left it on top of the wire crate that was part of the sleeping side. After about five, maybe ten, minutes, I realized what I had done and returned to retrieve the bag. When I first entered, all the puppies jumped up on the lattice in front of me and seemed so excited and happy. They apparently had quite the party pulling the bag off the crate and pulling all the tissue out of the bag, spreading it all around their pen. They acted like I had just left them the best present ever. It was not fun to do this job twice, but you have to smile and laugh at such adorable puppies.

At five weeks, we began taking the puppies outside. We built a fenced area on the grass about five by ten feet with a three-foot-high fence. I brought the puppies out two at a time and put them in the pen. I'd put bumpers and tennis balls in for them to explore and play with. They were so fun to watch and interact with. We were also observing all the puppies to see which one we wanted to keep. I'd love to keep them all, but that is not realistic for us. As we took them outside and introduced them to new things, we'd look for confidence, curiosity, and overall disposition. More and more, one guy kept standing out to us: Mr. Green.

Mr. Green always wanted to follow us, and his nose was always to the ground. His coloring was also darker yellow, which we wanted as it blends with the cattails better. And he looked like Mac. Mr. Green was also the noisiest of the puppies. He was always telling the others what they should be doing. One day, a friend was visiting the puppies while they were outside and I was working in our office. She came running to me rather concerned. "Maurita, one of the puppies is barking and chewing the other puppies' ears and jumping on them."

I knew without going to look. "Yeah, that's PJ. He's a busy, bossy boy."

"Oh." She walked back out to the puppies in deep contemplation.

Yes, we had decided to keep Mr. Green. His name would be MacHaven's Pepper Jack Chez because of his spicy personality and I wanted to have Mac and Chez (cheese). Originally his call name was to be Chez, but after working with his name awhile, it just wasn't flying. Mike came up with PJ, and that seemed to fit better.

At seven weeks, I allowed the puppies to be outside of the pen with Mac, Molly, and me. They watched Mac and Molly retrieve the bumpers and followed us around some of the trails. I was always counting puppies. I had to make sure I had all eight before moving on. We also got a kids' pool to introduce the puppies to water. It was a lot of fun watching them. Some hung over the edge, licking the water and putting their paws in. Others got right into it like PJ, Miss Red, and Mr. White. They all eventually got in and seemed to love it. On one of the outdoor adventures, Mr. Yellow got a hold of a big slug and was running around with it. I quickly ran after him to get him to drop it. In my attempt to get it out of his mouth, I ended up pushing it back, and he swallowed it. Yuck. As the veterinary receptionist said, "Yum, yum, extra protein." (Yes, I called the vet again. I figure better safe than sorry.) Another time, the adventurous puppies found a beehive in the ground along one of the trails. Three of them got stung: PJ, Mr. Blue, and Miss Red.

We needed to get the word out that we had puppies available. The Hiltons had changed Mac's registration, and the puppies could now be registered also. I made a poster with a picture of Mac and Molly, listing all their credentials, sires, dams, and clearances. Then I put the poster up around town. Our breeders also sent a few people our way. I prepared the puppy questionnaire for perspective puppy owners using one that Cheri used. We wanted good owners for our puppies and wouldn't sell them to anyone who wouldn't be responsible. By week 8, three of the puppies had been picked by approved families. On September 27, at nine weeks old, we loaded all eight of the puppies up, Mac and Molly too, and headed north to Cascade Kennels. There all the dogs would get their eyes checked and certified, and the puppies would get microchipped. Two of the families were going to pick their puppies up at the kennel. Mr. Blue, Baxter, was adopted by a wonderful family with a boy and girl to play with him. Miss Pink, Sachi, was adopted by a young man who guided people on fishing trips on our local rivers. Sachi was going to have a lot of adventures in the great outdoors. Miss Hot Pink, Jazz, was picked up by her family later at our home. She would have three young boys to play with her.

Miss Red, Mr. Yellow, Mr. Lime Green, and Mr. White stayed with us a while longer as we looked for good homes for them. Mr. Lime Green, Fraley, was next. He was adopted by a wonderful couple. The young man was a veteran and planned on hunting with Fraley. Then Mr. White, Wyatt, was adopted by a woman who adopted the puppy for her husband's birthday. Mr. Yellow and Miss Red stayed with us awhile longer, into the hunting season.

CHAPTER 18

Molly's First Hunt

Hunting season had arrived. Miss Red and Mr. Yellow were still with us in November for the first bird hunt of the season. We could not bring all the puppies, so we left all the puppies, including PJ, home with our critter sitter. Meanwhile Miss Red and Mr. Yellow needed names for training and our interaction with them. Miss Red became Mieko as this was a name Miss Pink's owner had considered and I liked it. Mr. Yellow became Mel as he was such a mellow guy.

We were excited to take Molly for her first hunt. Our friend Steve was with us. When my brother, Russ, got married and moved to Idaho, Steve took his place for our bird-hunting adventures. Steve's a good sport about sitting in the back of the truck with one of the dogs, even when they are wet. Maybe he doesn't have much of a choice, but he never complains. We loaded up our gear and food, said goodbye to the pups and the critter sitter, then headed off on our three-hour drive to Othello, Washington. It was cold and a little overcast, but it was not raining or snowing, and there wasn't much snow on the ground yet. However, it had been cold long enough that many of the ponds were frozen in Othello.

We arrived at our hunting spot, a field where ponds and cattails lie about its parameter. It always takes a little effort to get out of the comfy, cozy truck into the brisk cold, at least for me anyway. Maybe not for the boys or the dogs. They all have the excitement for the hunt pushing them. Mac and Molly were smelling the fields and wanted out of the truck. "You wait," I told them as I slid out of the truck. They pushed against me, wanting to get out. "Watch your nose," I lilted to them and waited for them to back up slightly to close the door. I zipped up my liner and made my way to the back of the truck where the boys were pulling out gear and shotguns.

My first priority was to open up the hand warmers to activate them. I put them in the pockets of my outer coat and found my water pack for me and the dogs. The outer coat went over the water pack. Gloves, hat, shells—and now we were ready to put the hunting collars on the dogs. "Back up," I told them as I opened the door just enough to slip in and put their collars on. Once on, I stood back, and Mac and Molly stepped forward. "Wait," they paused, and I smiled. "Okay." I opened the door fully, and they both leaped out of the truck.

We made our way to the cattails and ponds. Mac and Molly began working the fields with their noses to the ground. If they happen to jump a pheasant rooster, we can shoot it. But this morning, we were after ducks. We could hear ducks in the ponds as we approached. Even though we were on a hill above the ponds, we couldn't see them because of the cattails. Mike had a plan. "You two sit here with the dogs on this hillside. I'll work my way around and in to the cattails, causing them to fly up your way." Steve and I agreed and found a good spot to sit in the sagebrush with the dogs. Some geese flew overhead out of range. The dogs were focused looking to where they saw Mike enter the cattails. *Bang!* Steve and I struggled to stand as the dogs bolted off toward the shot.

"Well, that plan worked." Steve rolled his eyes and smiled as his gun rest in his arms.

"I got one down," Mike hollered up at us. "Let Mac go."

"He's already on his way. Call him. Molly's coming too." We heard Mike calling Mac and Molly then "Attaboy, Mac. Good boy!"

Then I heard Molly whining. "Mike, do you see Molly?"

"No, just Mac. The ice is thick. Maybe she couldn't bust through it."

I began calling Molly. *Toot, toot, toot!* "Here, Molly! Here, girl!" I paused and heard her whining. "Maybe she's hurt or stuck somewhere." My heart sank. Steve offered to make his way down through the cattails to find her. Meanwhile, I continued to call her, and she continued to whine. I watched Steve slowly work his way down through the cattails. I could see he does not feel the same urgency I feel. I could watch no longer. My baby girl was stuck or hurt. I kept calling her as I started to make my way down the hill through the cattails. Then she stopped whining. "Steve! Can you hear her? Can you see her?" I was starting to panic.

"Yes, she's up where we were sitting," Steve hollered back. I turned to head back and gave another whistle and call to Molly. I took about two steps, and here she came with a big smile. I dropped to my knee and gave her a big hug. "Good girl. I was worried about you."

Steve had made his way back up to me and Molly. We then made our way to where we thought Mike was. Just as we got to the bottom of the hill, here came Mike with duck in hand and Mac proudly walking next to him. "So what happened to the plan?" Steve made his way to Mike and Mac.

"As I came up to the pond, there were these ducks sitting there, quacking. I thought I might as well shoot one duck to get them to fly your way. But the few that were with him decided to fly the opposite way. They didn't cooperate." Steve patted Mike on the back and smiled. "Then as I was looking for where he fell, Mac came to me crashing through the ice. Molly must have got caught up and was unable to break through the ice."

"Aw, Molly. She wanted the duck so bad she whined, but not bad enough to push through that ice." I got down on my knee next to her and gave her another hug.

The rest of the day brought in a few more ducks, and Molly was able to make her retrieve and more. Steve had a great opportunity to shoot a rooster pheasant. The dogs flushed him right in front of Steve. You don't get a more perfect shot, but he missed. He gave some lame excuse. So we proudly welcomed him into our club that day, the CSWS club: Can't Shoot Worth … (you can add your own explanative).

Mike warming Molly after hunt.

CHAPTER 19

Training PJ

During December, we found homes for Mieko and Mel. Mel's new home was with a young family with a girl and boy who began loving him the moment they saw him. They liked the name Mel and kept it. Mieko's new family was a young man and his grandfather. They changed her name to Blitz. The young man was an EMT (emergency medical technician) working evenings. He and his grandfather were going to split their time taking care of Blitz. I felt pretty good about all the families we found for our puppies, although it was very hard to let them go.

Now we were three. Training for Mac and Molly continued as before, but PJ needed to start at the beginning. So I signed us up for a basic puppy class at the local pet store. There were two puppy classes. One was for puppies six to eight months old, and the other, eight months to a year. PJ was seven months old. Because of his spicy personality and I'd already been working with him, I wanted to put him in the class for eight months to a year. The gal at the counter signing us up got the trainer and told her my wishes. The trainer then came over to me and PJ and was insistent that PJ be in the class for six to eight months old. I objected but eventually relented.

The following Wednesday, I loaded PJ up, and we went to the pet store for our first class. It seemed like PJ felt special that he was going for a ride in the car without the other two. He sat in the front seat and looked over at me periodically. We got there ten minutes early so I could let PJ do his business before class and let him walk around the store a bit before class. PJ was very excited and pulling to sniff everything possible. I let him explore for a bit then persisted to pull him in the direction of the class. The area for the class was a five-by-ten-foot area defined by benches with an opening to walk into. There were about five ladies with their puppies, all small breeds. PJ was twice the size of the largest puppy there. The trainer invited us in, asking our names and checking us off her list. I brought PJ in and sat down. Right away, PJ started showing the small puppies who was boss. I pulled PJ close, and he kept pulling and barking at the other puppies. The owners all grabbed their puppies and put them in their laps. I worked to get PJ to sit, but he wasn't complying.

"Okay, well, I think PJ would do better with some older puppies," the trainer said with a smile.

"I tried to tell you that," I replied defensively.

"Yes, well, I see now. Tell the gal at the counter I told you to switch. There is no fee. We'll see you tomorrow." She turned to the remaining ladies with their puppies. "Now there is no bad puppy. Sometimes you just need to make the right matches." Although vindicated, I was also embarrassed and frustrated she wouldn't listen to me initially.

PJ and I returned the next day for the older-puppy class. This went much better, although the trainer did need to settle PJ down at the beginning of the class by holding him by the scruff of the neck while she calmly talked about what we would learn in the class and what we could expect. PJ calmed down within a minute, and she returned him to me to have him sit by me. We did our eight weeks of classes and received our certificate. PJ did well and enjoyed the classes. He interacted well with the other dogs after the first class. During an exercise, he even helped another dog that was fearful walking in the store. He sat down next to the dog, and it responded to PJ, relaxed, and lay down. Dogs are truly amazing.

PJ was a very busy boy. He was always finding things to get into. One day, as I was working in the office, I heard a dog running up the stairs and then jumping up and down off the bed. I looked up; Molly was lying down next to me. I walked out to the living room, and Mac was lying on the couch. "PJ? Where are you, puppy?" No response. I worked my way up the stairs and looked into the bedroom. There was PJ, standing in the middle of the bed with Mike's bottle of Desenex in his mouth, wagging his tail, so happy and proud of his find. There was a trail of powder across the bed, onto the floor, into the closet, looping back up and down on the bed several more times. "Oh, PJ!" I sighed. I couldn't help but smile; he was so cute and so pleased with himself. "Fetch it here, puppy." PJ let me take it from him. "Good boy." Never scold a retriever for retrieving. I leaned toward him for a kiss. "Pee-ew! Maybe kisses aren't such a good idea right now. But you're a good boy." I pat PJ on his head. Desenex breath is not appealing like normal puppy breath.

Another puppy kiss not as desirable is after he's consumed poop. Yes, unfortunately, PJ acquired the habit of poop eating. It doesn't matter how fresh as long as it's solid. We had a stretch of freezing temperatures, and water was freezing around the shore of the pond and lake. I returned from letting the dogs out to brush my teeth, and the dogs bounded up the stairs to Mike, who was already in bed. "Maurita," Mike hollered down to me.

"Yeah," I replied with the toothbrush now in my mouth.

"Could you come up here?" He sounded dismayed. I put my toothbrush down and gave my mouth a quick rinse.

"What is it?"

"PJ brought a frozen poop up into the bed," he replied with disgust.

I laughed. "Great!" I went to get a couple of paper towels in the kitchen. I ran up the stairs to the bedroom. "Well, at least it's frozen." Mike rolled his eyes at me as I picked the poop up with the paper towels. "There, you can't even tell. Do you want a new pillowcase?"

"Nah, that's okay, hon," Mike replied as he turned his pillow to the other side and plopped back down on his pillow.

Then there was the PJ and crown 7 (Seagram's) incident. The vet had given me a bottle of Betadine solution to treat Mac's paw that had gotten cut by a piece of glass on a trail. Every morning, I would add water to a bit of the solution and soak Mac's foot for a few minutes. The solution was the consistency and color of iodine. After our walk that morning, I treated Mac's foot and set the solution on the counter in the laundry room. It was a beautiful spring day, and I was going to leave the dogs inside while we worked out in the yard. After a couple of hours, I came inside to get some water and check on the dogs. Mac and Molly greeted me at the door, wagging their tails in their normal fashion. Where was PJ? I walked into the living room, and there was PJ, lying on the carpet with the bottle of Betadine solution in his mouth dripping onto the carpet. He had been walking when the cap first popped off from his chewing so there was a line leading to where he turned around to lie down and then a puddle as he lay there with the solution dripping onto the carpet. The end result was, he had created a 7 with a little pool at the top that looked like a crown on top. It wouldn't clean up completely, so we had a 7 with a crown on our carpet for a year or so. It eventually wore off, and you can't see it anymore.

Mr. Nose, as we sometimes call him, also seems to be very sensitive. He senses things, like when our daughter-in-law was pregnant. It was the first time she visited us since she became pregnant. We were sitting in the living room, talking, when PJ quietly came up to her, sniffed, then stepped onto the couch to sniff her belly. Then he looked at her, backed quietly off the couch, and lay back down with Mac and Molly. Dogs are amazing.

CHAPTER 20

More Puppies?

I wasn't actively pursuing breeding Mac, but it was still in the back of my mind. PJ was a year old now and had experienced his first hunting season. Mac, of course, continued to be the master hunter, and the young ones, as I began referring to Molly and PJ, were learning from him. With another hunting season behind us, it was time to catch up at home. I was checking e-mail, and a friend had sent me a post from her place of employment. Someone was looking to breed their yellow female Labrador within the next few months. Such a wonderful finding! I really want to breed Mac. He is so good-looking, and his temperament is exceptional. So I replied to the e-mail, giving Mac's credentials and clearances on eyes, hips, elbows, and heart, along with recent pictures of Mac, Molly, and PJ.

We received an e-mail back.

> Hi, I am Chuck Lucus, Mary's husband and fellow Lab lover. We are not traditional breeders, but we do have a new litter every two or three years. We currently have three Labs—Ivory, Zoe, and Chloe. Our Labs are little females fifty to sixty pounds. We are looking for a male as white or light as possible and as small as possible. Chloe

was the result of breeding Zoe to a line of Labs imported from Sweden. We have champions and a master hunter in the lineage, but it's their unique personalities we seek. We do not breed for profit but continue the line. We always have people just waiting for our pups. We expect Chloe to come into heat sometime in March, so we need to find a soul mate soon. How much does your Lab weigh? Could we arrange soon to come and see him in person with our girls? What do you charge for stud service? We are used to giving pick of the litter excepting the smallest female, which Mary always seems to pick for our brood.

Could this really be happening? I could hardly wait for Mike to come home from work and to share the news. We were going to breed Mac! Mike was excited about the news but more patient. There was a lot more exchange of information needed, and then we needed to meet the female and her owners. So we replied,

Hello, Chuck! We have only bred Mac once to our female, Molly. We feel Mac is an awesome dog and would like to continue the line that our breeders, the Hiltons, did so well at. They have recently retired from breeding. Molly and Mac's litter in 2008 was our first litter. Mac's stud fee is $700. We live in Enumclaw. Molly is around sixty-two pounds, and Mac is eighty-one pounds. We had eight puppies that varied in size and shades of yellow. PJ, whom we kept, was the darkest and smallest. He is 1.5 years and six-ty-four pounds. I've attached a couple of recent puppy pictures. We would love to have you come meet Mac, and we could meet your females. The Hiltons live in Snohomish, and it takes about 1.5

hours to get there. Our schedule is often flexible, and we can work something out weekdays or weekends. Thank you! Hope to meet you soon! Mike and Maurita Motland.

It was four days, and we had not received a reply. I was concerned they had decided against using Mac. Maybe they found a different Lab. On the fifth day, we received a reply.

Beautiful pups! Question—would you consider "pick of the litter" in lieu of stud fee? Would you consider "trading" stud services with one of our males in our litter for your Molly?

Yes! We were still on. Our reply,

We would consider pick of the litter in lieu of stud fee. I was actually just thinking about that yesterday. Molly has been spayed (sadly).

We then worked out the details to meet that Saturday. They were coming to our place with their females to meet us and Mac. I could hardly wait. That's two days away!

Saturday was sunny and not too cold for the end of January. I was glad we had chores to keep busy with while we waited for our expected visitors to arrive. The dogs started barking, and I looked up to see our visitors drive up our driveway. I put the broom and dustpan away in the closet as Mike went out to greet them. "You guys wait for now. Don't worry. You'll get to meet them," I told the pups as I squeezed by them to go out the door. Mary and Chuck were probably about our age and had five Labs with them, their three females and two visiting puppies. The five Labs piled out of their van and immediately started playing and chasing one another. We shook hands and greeted one another while Mac, Molly, and PJ barked and protested inside the house.

"Would you like to see our dogs now?" I asked, starting toward the door.

"Yes, please let them out," Chuck replied.

So I did. Three very excited Labradors bounded out to see what was happening in their yard. Mac and Molly settled down and were sniffing the other dogs and Mary and Chuck. PJ was a bit more adamant about making sure everyone knew this was his place. He barked excitedly and tried to chase the other dogs. "Why don't you put him on a leash?" Mike suggested to me.

"Yeah, okay." I hurried in and got the leash, then collected PJ, and clipped the leash on his collar. It took him a moment to settle down.

"Well, that is not desirable behavior," Mary snipped.

"Yes, we're working on it." I apologized. *Ugh*, I thought, hoping this wouldn't change their minds about Mac.

Mary and Chuck liked our property and the kennel we would use for Mac and Chloe to bond as "soul mates." Mary gave us more papers for Chloe and more pictures, a whole CD worth of pictures. I thought I took a lot of pictures. "So everything looks good. We'll keep you posted as to Chloe coming into heat." Mary smiled and collected the copies of Mac's papers.

"We plan on doing one more test for Mac next week. It's for EIC. We'll send you the results as soon as we get them." I hated to say it, but we had to do it. It would be totally irresponsible to go forward with breeding Mac and not know for certain.

"Great. Thank you." Mary did not seem concerned. I was still hopeful.

CHAPTER 21

The Results

When Mac had his first and only episode in question, testing for EIC was invasive and expensive. Now a simple blood sample can be taken by your vet and mailed to the testing laboratory in Minnesota. It's not as expensive but still expensive for our budget. We needed to do it, so we took Mac in to the vet. She took the sample, then we mailed it with special packaging to keep the sample cool and protected, and the special delivery to get it there by that afternoon was also costly. But we did it. Now we waited for the results.

The package was sent on Tuesday, and that Friday, we had the results in our e-mail.

> Hello Mr. and Mrs. Motland, we recently tested your dog Mac for exercise-induced collapse. His test came back affected. Please let me know if you would like me to send his result to OFA (Orthopedic Foundation for Animals), and I will get that taken care of right away. For further tests, please note that you can use the result report (as attached) for submission and you should not send OFA applications or fees with samples.

Thank you, and please let me know if you have any questions.

Katie Minor

Not the answer I was hoping for, but I guess we knew it all along. I guess we were just doing a good job of monitoring Mac since we never had another episode. Not good for the breeding plan, however. I had hoped that maybe he was just a carrier. A carrier can have symptoms, but they are a better option for breeding. As I read over the explanation of genotypes from the university, it appeared to be possible to breed Mac as long as the female didn't have the EIC form of the gene. She would be clear. Chuck and Mary, however, did not agree, saying that the gene would still be passed on from Mac and show up later down the line.

So everything stopped. No more hunt tests, no future possibility of showing Mac or PJ. We had Molly fixed a year after the puppies. Mike wasn't willing to go through having Molly in heat or a litter of puppies again. Even though I did most of the daily work, it was still an imposition on everyone in the home. Now Mac, Molly, and PJ are just our faithful, wonderful companions who love to go everywhere with us, especially to hunt birds.

CHAPTER 22

Back to Daily Work

Nothing changed much really. Hunting has always been the primary job for our pups. Daily exercise and training to do this job continues. This requires me to work also to be their calm, assertive pack leader. We knew we should get Mac fixed, but we continued to struggle financially and hoped to put it off until we could afford the operation. I was still holding on to some hope that we could breed PJ.

I began to notice a slight change in Mac's gait as he would run to retrieve his bumpers. He was still an all-out guy, but it seemed he was holding his right rear leg slightly. Nothing real obvious, but I wanted to keep an eye on him. After our morning walks, the boys would settle out in the living room on the couch, and Molly would follow me out to the office. She would lie down as I worked. Every time I got up to file something or go to the bathroom, Molly got up and followed me. She was my shadow.

This one morning, PJ, always needing something to do, decided to try to get Mac to play with him. Mac was lying on the end of the couch. PJ barked at Mac and talked to him, stepping up on the couch, pawing at him. This was actually a normal occurrence, except this morning—Mac was answering back. We've always tried to have the young ones respect Mac, and as he was getting older, it seemed to be more important. This morning, perhaps I was a bit tired, maybe stressed about work. I don't know, but I decided that that was enough. PJ had to stop annoying Mac this way, and I was going to do something about it right now.

I marched out there. "I have had enough of this, young man." I grabbed PJ by the scruff and put him down on the floor on his side. Hindsight—Mac was not annoyed, and they were having a perfectly healthy interaction. Note to self—never correct your dog in annoyance and/or frustration. Nothing good comes of it. Indeed, to my surprise, Mac bounded off the couch and joined in with me correcting PJ, growling at him and trying to bite him. PJ responded in defense. I was totally taken back and horrified. My boys were fighting, growling, and barking fiercely. I grabbed each of them by their scruffs to hold them at bay until I could catch my breath. I got them to lie down, and I sat on the floor between them trying to figure out what I did wrong. Molly calmly entered in and joined me, lying down between the boys. Just when you think you know your dog, they surprise you. I was amazed at Molly's calm response. She didn't run in fear, nor did she join in the fight.

When Mike got home from work, I told him what had happened. "Uh-oh, sounds like we need to move up the time for Mac's surgery," he responded solemnly. That evening, it became apparent that we needed to keep Mac and PJ separate or nobody would be getting any sleep. I went and got one of the dog crates out of the garage. We set it up in the kitchen with PJ's bedding in it. "Sorry, buddy. I don't like this, but we got to get some sleep. Kennel up," I commanded. PJ complied. The next few days, it was a continual effort to keep Mac and PJ from fighting. I tried to be the confident pack leader, leading them back to a happy pack, but was failing miserably.

One morning, in my effort to separate the boys, my arm got in the way, and I got bit. I had a sweatshirt and coat on, so I only got a huge bruise with a couple of punctures. The electronic collar worn by PJ also got punctured, and they drew blood on each other. I was calling and messaging everyone I knew in the dog world for advice on how to handle this. I really wanted to leave PJ intact, but it was looking more and more like this would not be possible. Just two days before this all started, I had taken a picture of Mac and PJ sleeping, snuggled together next to me while I was working. What happened? PJ would be two in July. Did his hormones kick in?

I messaged a friend on Facebook who breeds bloodhounds. She has both males and females, which she shows and breeds. I told her what had happened. She replied,

> Wow, Maurita, drawing blood is getting serious, but the wound you received has me most concerned. I absolutely cannot say we are without fights here, and I have had a lot of households in my classes with multiple dogs and fighting. What I can tell you is that from my experience, it is essential that, first and foremost, the dogs realize you are in control. If I have a dogfight, I can yell "Knock it off," and they may not stop growling, but they separate. I have had some pretty gnarly fights (having multiple intact boys and girls in season), but the dogs respect me and usually can be separated without actually putting myself in a position to get hurt. If I have to, I will throw a metal bowl in their general direction, and it separates the fight. Let me know if you have specific questions, but I would really suggest incorporating some rigorous obedience training just to help establish/remind them of your place in the family and eliminating freedoms if they are not respectful of you. Hope this helps.

Do my dogs respect me? Right now, I'm thinking not, but maybe more is happening with Mac than I realize. When dogs are in pain, they sometimes respond more aggressively. We got both Mac and PJ in for their surgery on the same day. There was one more big fight after their surgery. Mike was home and was downstairs when it happened. I was upstairs with the dogs fussing with them when it happened. Mike ran up the stairs when he heard the fight. He grabbed Mac, and I grabbed PJ. It was somewhat helpful that they were both recovering from surgery. I kept the boys separated by a gate in the kitchen when we couldn't be with them. We'd put Molly with Mac one time and then with PJ the next. I also purchased muzzles for them both. When we took walks or let them out to relieve themselves, we put the muzzles on. After a few weeks, they settled down. We no longer needed to separate them, nor were the muzzles required. Thank you, Lord, we're a happy family once again.

CHAPTER 23

Aging Begins

Mac was nine years old and definitely slowing down. We gave him Deramaxx, an anti-inflammatory, when he showed pain, and that helped him. In spite of arthritis and pain, Mac still played hard and with full heart. He has always been an all-out boy. When retrieving a bumper or bird in water, he leaped off the shore with a huge splash. Retrieving on land, he pounced on that bumper or bird with full gusto. This often led to sore muscles and joints, especially after a full day of hunting.

After the surgery, Mac put on some weight. He was always up for bumpers in the morning, but in the afternoon, when I'd take them out, he'd walk out and lie down on the grass. Something was not right, but I couldn't put my finger on it. It didn't seem that his age should be a factor yet. I was talking to Molly's breeder, Cheri, about Mac, and she suggested it could be hypothyroidism. "I'll send you an article on it. Be sure to have your vet test Mac for it." So on Mac's next visit to the vet, we had him tested, and he was diagnosed with hypothyroidism, an underactive thyroid gland. Treatment is a pill given every twelve hours. The a.m. pill was added to his meal, and the evening pill was wrapped in some cheese or meat, depending on what we were having for dinner. Of course, the other two got the treat also, minus the pill.

Mac was back to his energetic self. Although arthritis was still a factor, it didn't slow him down much. His weight came down, and all was well. When we walk and play with bumpers, each dog has to have their own bumper. I don't want them stealing from one another because I don't want them playing tug-of-war with a bird. One game I enjoyed with the dogs is to set up to have them race for their bumpers. I would leave the bumpers in an open area and take the dogs for a walk. When we came around to a straight run to the bumpers, I'd send all three to the bumpers. They loved racing one another to the bumpers. When Mac was younger, I had to put four bumpers out because Mac would always grab two, sometimes even three leaving Molly or PJ without a bumper. Now the young ones outrun Mac, so they are sure to get theirs and Mac gets his too.

The weekend before Labor Day weekend, we were out working on our trails, cutting back blackberries, and weed eating. It was a beautiful sunny day, and the dogs were out with us exploring. Mac was eating grass. That boy loved to eat grass. The other two eat it also, but not as much as Mac. Later, as we came inside, Mac seemed to be drooling excessively. We weren't certain what caused that but kept an eye on him. By dinnertime, he appeared normal, and the drooling had stopped. Labor Day weekend is usually a weekend of labor for us. More trail work was needed, and it was looking like the weather was going to cooperate with us. On Saturday morning, we were awakened by the dogs and the usual snuggling and dog kisses on the bed. PJ and Molly always get in there first, then we make room for Mac. I called Mac over. He came to my side of the bed. I reached down to pet him, and his whole body went stiff, and he fell to his side.

I cried out to Mike. He came over, and we both tried to steady his body as he began to convulse. "Jesus," I cried, "help our puppy!" Both Mike and I prayed for the convulsing to stop and for Mac to be okay. After a couple of minutes, the convulsing stopped. Mac got up and was a bit confused and wobbly. He jumped up on the bed, ran across, and then jumped off the other side. His bowels let loose, and he had an accident as he ran across. He was intent on getting outside, so I ushered all the dogs out for the usual morning duties. Mac had a seizure! Was it something he ate? What caused it? We kept an eye on him all weekend. There were no more incidents, and he appeared to be normal.

As Monday was a holiday, I called the vet first thing Tuesday morning and was able to get him in to see the vet. The vet checked him over and asked a lot of questions. Mac had a grand mal seizure. The excessive drooling the prior weekend could have been a minor one. "What causes them?" I asked the vet.

"Well, given his age, it could be the hypothyroidism, a tumor, or a brain infection. We can give him phenobarbital to suppress the seizures if he has a lot of them. At this point, we need to wait and watch him. If he has seizures in clusters or an isolated seizure once a month or more, then we should consider the phenobarbital." She then gave me information on seizures, types, causes, when to medicate, and the side effect of the medication.

Mac and I paid our bill and walked out to the car, where Molly and PJ awaited us, tails wagging as they looked out through the nose-smudged windows. I was quiet and deep in thought as I loaded Mac up. Maybe he ate something that caused this. I began to consider all the different kinds of vegetation on our property. He spends so much time grazing on grass maybe he got something bad with the grass. There was one plant in the area he was eating grass in that I don't like. It has nasty seeds that cover you and the dogs when you walk through. I was going to research this plant. Maybe it was the culprit.

On our next walk, I picked a sample of the plant and dug out our plant books. After much time spent looking at pictures, comparing the plant to the pictures and the description given regarding the leaves, the roots, the flowers, I determined that plant was Douglas's water hemlock, extremely poisonous if ingested. Even small amounts can be deadly to both humans and livestock. All parts of the plant are poisonous, but the roots and stem base especially so. The basal parts of one plant can kill a cow. Signs of poisoning: nervousness, excessive salvation and frothing, muscle twitching, dilation of the pupils, and grand mal seizures.

That's it. I was convinced. Now to keep Mac out of those areas until we can eradicate it! I knew I hated those plants. They grow in the grass that Mac so loved to eat around the pond and by the lake. In spite of our efforts, Mac continued to have seizures every two to six months. They typically happened around 5:00 a.m., and he would throw up grass first. I, or both Mike and I, would hold him so he wouldn't hurt himself. "Not too tight," Mike told me one time. "You'll choke him." I loosened my hold but still held him firmly.

We did everything to live life as normal as possible. Mac was still the master hunter in our pack. One November weekend, we started with an upland hunt on Friday at Gloyd Seeps in eastern Washington, a public area with rolling hills and ponds with creeks littered throughout. It was a crisp, beautiful sunny day. The dogs were very excited. It was a wonderful day out with all the pups, but no birds were flying. Heading back to the truck, Mac flushed a rooster out of the cattails. Mike hollered, "Rooster," and *bang!* He shot; the bird fell into the cattails. All the dogs went in to find the bird. Who came out with the bird? Mac. "Good boy! We're not skunked." Great day, and the pups were all very happy.

We headed to the hotel to eat, go to bed, and rise early for hunting at Linda Lake in Othello, our standby. It's a public area, so 4:30 a.m. wake-up time is necessary to get to our spot. In spite of hitting the snooze button a time or two, we got there early enough to get our spot. We decided to take all three dogs instead of taking turns and leaving two in the truck. I really like them all being there. We loaded up the gear and hauled it down to the lake with the dogs running circles around us. We got the decoys all set up and settled in to the blind. It was about twenty-five degrees and somewhat clear. You sweat bringing all the gear down then have to layer up as you sit waiting for the ducks.

Shortly after settling in, six coots slowly swam toward us. We hesitated as we've never shot coots before. In fact, this was the first time we'd seen them at Linda Lake. Mac got impatient and could no longer wait. He broke out in pursuit of the coots, with Molly close behind. We all stood up, and Mike decided to shoot one for the dogs. PJ jumped in after that one and retrieved the dead coot. Mac and Molly continued in pursuit of the swimming coots. "No, Mac! No, Molly! No bird!" I hollered, followed by the whistle and "Here!" PJ came into the blind with the coot, and we helped him into the blind. I recently learned that an EIC episode can happen in water. I hadn't realized that as Mac seemed to be more heat affected. Both Mike and I were hollering at Mac and Molly, but they kept following after those coots, occasionally barking at them. As I was getting more concerned for Mac, I realized that all the hollering was excitement to Mac and Molly, pushing them further in the chase—the opposite of what we wanted. They were about halfway across the lake at this point, chasing those miserable coots. I wasn't worried about Molly. She was the swimming queen and very strong and didn't have EIC episodes, which could be brought on by all this excitement. I dropped to me knees and started to pray, "Jesus, please help my puppies." Steve was watching the dogs with the binoculars. The coots were still swimming just out of reach of both dogs. Mike continued to call the dogs.

Finally, Molly turned and began to swim back. "Good girl! Good girl, Molly!" Mike called to her. I continued to pray and looked up to see Mac. He continued across the lake. At this point, it was closer for him to continue to the shore on the other side. "Okay, good boy," I told myself. "Just get to the shore quickly. We'll figure out how to get you." I know Mac. He likes to shorten his swim distance and runs the bank, which gives him lower scores in hunt test, but that was smart of him. He finally reached the other side. I released a huge sigh. Mac already had a plan. I should know that. I've got Steve's binoculars now to watch Mac. Mac ran the bank and started swimming to an island that's down from the blind. That would shorten his swim. He reached the island and ran the shore to the other side. I lost sight of him. My stomach turned. I continued praying, "Please, God, help my puppy." He reappeared out of some brush. "Thank you! Thank you!" I whispered.

As we saw Mac's plan, Mike and I began to make our way down the shore toward the island. Mac jumped in the water and started swimming to our side of the lake. Finally, he reached the shore and started back toward us. "Good boy, Mac! Oh, puppy, good boy!" We were almost in tears; we were so relieved and happy. Now to head back to the blind. We had actually come quite a ways down from the blind. Linda Lake is a huge mudhole. Coming down, we had adrenaline to help us. Heading back was now slow and difficult. Both Mike and I were struggling, finding every hole that we somehow missed on the way out. Mike's foot got stuck in the muck, and he took a dunk, getting his sleeves wet. We made it back to the blind, and Mike decided he needed to change his coat and gloves. So he took Mac and Molly back to the truck. He changed his coat and gloves and loaded Mac and Molly up in the truck. "You guys had enough excitement. You take a break."

So PJ got some solo time. It was a good confidence builder for him. He got to retrieve another coot and a duck that Steve shot. After an hour or so, the action slowed, and we were getting cold. Mike and Steve decided to take all the dogs for a walk to warm up. Maybe the dogs would flush a rooster. I stayed in the blind with our gear. Maybe a duck would come in. It is so peaceful sitting in the blind. I don't mind sitting there by myself, and my hand warmers were doing a fair job at keeping me warm. It hadn't been very long when Mike radioed me. "Nanny Goat, this is Mountain Goat 5."

"Yeah, go ahead, 5."

"PJ and Molly each flushed a hen. Mac was hunting hard and disappeared in some cattails. I can't see him, and I can't get him to come."

"What!" We barely got this boy back to safety, and now they couldn't find him? I about jumped out of the blind. "I'll come help you find him."

"Okay. Steve said he saw him about a quarter mile away, up by the highway."

My heart sank. I got up and started heading toward the area I figured the boys had gone. *Toot, toot, toot!* I whistled. "Hey, hey, hey! Here, Mac! Here, Mac!"

I was trying to remain strong and calm for Mac, but I was panicking. Thoughts were running through my head: *Did he col-*

lapse? Did someone pick him up? Did he get hit by a car? I was pushing through the tall grass, whistling, and calling Mac without rest. Finally, I saw Steve, and then beyond him, I saw Mac. "Thank you, Jesus. My baby's okay." I called Mac, and he passed by Steve, making his way to me. When he reached me, tail wagging, I dropped to my knee to draw him close. I was so happy to see him. "Good boy! You're such a good boy, Mac!" He looked at me as I drew him close, and it seemed he realized this was a big deal. He leaned into me.

CHAPTER 24

Senior Moments

Other than the seizures—and they were occurring once every three to four months (not monthly)—Mac was doing well. We managed his arthritis with daily glucosamine in his food and Deramaxx (anti-inflammatory) as needed. He did seem to be wandering more. I couldn't figure out if he truly couldn't hear when we called him or if he just gets off into his own world of scents and all else fades away. He certainly could hear a food wrapper being opened in the pantry from anywhere in the house. He would come running. More and more, off in his senior moment, he ignored our calling him for twenty minutes or more.

One morning, I took all three for their morning walk and swim. It was a beautiful day, so after our walk, I had them lie down in the grass while I started weeding the garden. I looked up periodically to count dogs. *One, two, three.* I smiled. They were all lying in the shade. I went back to weeding. I looked up again. It couldn't have been more than a minute since the last check. Where's Mac? PJ grabbed his bumper as he saw me look their way, hoping for some playtime. "Mac? Here, Mac! Where are you?" I checked some tall grassy areas close by that he often wanders into. No Mac. I put Molly and PJ inside and proceeded to walk the property, calling for Mac. Twenty-four acres seems like fifty when your fur baby is nowhere in sight. Or maybe he's in trouble? I checked all his favorite places, calling him. I checked by the lake, by the pond, in the new growth where deer poop abounds (he liked to snack on it). No Mac.

My worse fear is that he would have a seizure or an EIC episode, get caught somewhere, and not be able to come to us. I started back toward the house feeling dejected and without hope. As I neared the house, I heard Mike holler "He's here! Mac is here!" I came up to the house, and there he was, lying by the front porch in the grass, panting, wet, mud on his feet and nose. I really wish I had a camera on that boy to see where he went and what he got into. "Aw, Mac, you stinker. Come on, let's dry you off." So glad he was safe, again.

Another time, some friends had dropped by just after we had finished the morning walk. I kept trying to count dogs as I listened and conversed with our friends. *One, two—no Mac.* "Excuse me. I need to call my dog."

"No problem." They stopped for me to call Mac. "Here, Mac! Here!" They proceeded to talk. I interrupted a few more times to call Mac. Still no sight of Mac. Finally, I blurted, "I'm sorry, I have to go look for Mac." I started to break away on the search, and who appeared up at the top of the hill? Mac, standing proud, holding something in his mouth.

"Well, there he is," my friend offered. "What does Mac have in his mouth?" It was brown and looked like a duck body without a head or wings.

"Oh dear, I'm not sure," I offered to our friends. "Good boy, Mac! Here, buddy! Fetch it here," I called feeling a bit reluctant to find out what delightful thing he had found. He came bounding down the hill toward us, proud to show us what he had found. As he got close, I sighed with relief. "It's a football! You found an old, deflated football!"

During a visit from Mike's mom, we were out walking with the dogs, showing Grace how the water levels were up as they do every fall and winter. The levels of the lake and pond were way up and filled in the backfield. It was a cloudy and somewhat cool day. We had on light jackets and jeans. Heading back to the house, I saw

Molly and PJ but no Mac. "Here, Mac! Come on, boy! This way!" I kept calling him as we walked back to the house. We got back to the house, and still no Mac. I grabbed the whistle and headed back out to find Mac. I walked back to where we had last seen Mac, calling and whistling for him. I reached the lake, and there was Mac, treading water with a big stick in his mouth. The water level was up to the lower branches of the cedar, and it looked like he was caught on the cedar branches. I had no idea how long he's been stuck there treading water and trying to bring us that stick. "Oh, Mac." I didn't give it a second thought. I took off my coat and dropped it on the ground. I was hoping that I would only have to get wet up to my waist to get to him. The hill dropped off steeper than I thought. I had to swim to reach him. I reached for Mac's belly to give him a lift over the branch. He was then able to swim into shore. Mac shook the water off and wagged his tail at me. I grabbed my coat, and we headed back to the house, Mac with his stick, me dripping wet and shivering. As I came up to the house, Mike opened the garage door. He greeted me with his eyes wide. "What do you need me to do?"

"Could you dry Mac off?"

Grace peeked into the garage. "Can I get you anything?"

"Yes, could you bring me a towel from the bathroom?" She hurried off and returned with a towel. I removed my wet clothes and put them in the sink, then wrapped up in the towel, and rushed upstairs to dress in some warm clothes. "Mac, what I do for you, buddy." Once again Mac, was safe with us.

CHAPTER 25

Not Ready to Retire

September 26, 2014, Mac would be twelve years old. Just over a month away. He still loved his walks, swims, bumpers and was always ready to play. I had toyed with the idea of retiring him from hunting to minimize the potential for injuries, but Mac wasn't having any of that. Anytime we'd leave him in the truck and he didn't get to hunt, he would protest profusely.

Mac had started sneezing this summer. I decided it was due to allergies, although he'd never had them before. The sneezing, however, became more frequent and engaged his full body. Sometimes he'd hit his head on the floor. On a warm summer afternoon walk, Mac did one of those sneezes. Mike was the first to notice that he had hit his nose on the ground so hard it was bleeding. We got everyone back to the house so we could look at Mac closer. We cleaned his nose up and saw that the bleeding had stopped, something we're going to have to watch for the boy. The sneezes gradually became more frequent and more violent. We began following Mac closely so we could bend down and hold him up when he sneezed, keeping him from hitting his nose on the ground. One day, I came back from running errands, my arms full of groceries, and the dogs were swarming around me, wagging their tails. One of the tails got Mac's nose, which prompted a sneeze attack. I rushed to put the groceries down and get back to Mac. It was too late. His nose was bleeding, and blood splattered all over the wall and on the floor. "Oh, baby. I'm so sorry." I got some tissue and bent down to clean his nose. He kissed me and wagged his tail.

We couldn't keep this up. I called the vet and was able to get him in the next day. The vet was able to see a bump inside his right nostril. They recommended administering anesthesia so they could get a good sample to send to the lab to test for cancer. Two days later, we were to bring Mac back for the procedure. We were hoping and praying it was not cancerous. All went well, and they were able to get a good sample. In fact, the vet was so excited they were able to get a good sample she took a picture, which she showed me when I came to pick Mac up. "Look. It was close to his nostril opening and very reachable. We got a great sample to send to the lab." I tried to be serious and not show the amusement I felt that this vet was so excited about this lump in my dog's nostril. Please, just let it not be cancerous.

The results came back positive for cancer. They referred us to a veterinary oncologist. We weren't able to get an appointment with her until September 29, one month after the diagnosis. The treatment options were radiation treatment for four weeks at a clinic at Washington State University in Pullman, Washington. The cost for the treatment would be around $4,000. In addition, there would be the travel and accommodation costs. Side effects to the radiation are skin and mouth irritation/burns. She e-mailed a report after the appointment, which read "Without treatment, the tumor progresses over a few months. The main problems are related to nose bleeding and congestion of the nose leading to the decision of euthanasia. An anti-inflammatory medication can be used to decrease inflammation and increase comfort of the patient, but this is a very conservative treatment that will not significantly prolong the life of the patient, if used as the only form of treatment."

Without radiation therapy, the oncologist gave Mac two and a half months to live. She said the burn from radiation is like a pizza burn in the roof of your mouth. We have a friend who had radiation treatment on his throat. That wasn't a small pizza burn. It was a horrible burn, and he was miserable for a month or more. Mac just turned twelve years old. We just couldn't see putting him through the radiation treatment. So we opted for the anti-inflammatory and lots of daily prayer.

CHAPTER 26

One Day at a Time

Mac didn't seem to know he only had two and a half months to live. The anti-inflammatory was working. Mac stopped sneezing, and the medication also helped with the arthritis. We were encouraged. Hunting was in a month, and Mac was ready to go. He hunted strong that season, turned thirteen the following September, a whole year after the diagnosis of two and a half months.

For this next hunting season, we decided to hunt the dogs one at a time. This would ensure Mac got a break and didn't overdo. It would also be good for the young ones to get one-on-one attention.

We were duck hunting on Frenchman's Wasteway near Othello, Washington. It was PJ's turn to hunt. We each had set up on a hill at the waterway. PJ and I were lower and closer to the water, tucked in some cattails. It was overcast and not too cold. I was adjusting PJ's neoprene vest when *bang!* Steve shot a duck, and it fell in the cattails just behind PJ and me. "Okay, PJ, hunt it up!" PJ worked hard to find that bird, but the cattails were thick, and his inexperience worked against him. We had lost a couple in this area yesterday. After all of us looking for a while, Mike decided to go get Mac and Molly. Three dogs searching for the bird should bring better results.

Mac and Molly were excited and barking as Mike approached the truck. They had heard the gunshot earlier, and here came Papa. Mike opened the door. "Okay, pups." Mac didn't waste anytime. He jumped out of the truck, ran up the hill, stopped, and gave Mike a quick look, then he was off toward the blinds, with Molly close behind.

I saw them coming, Mac leading the way down the trail to us. "Hunt 'em up!" I hollered, but it wasn't necessary. They both started working the area. Within a minute, Mac came up with the bird. The pro. The master. He was so pleased, and so were we. Mac to the rescue.

Every morning and every night, we snuggle the dogs. We pray for Mac for healing and strength. I believe God is answering our prayers. It's been over a year since he was diagnosed with cancer, and he just finished his second hunting season since that diagnosis. One night, Mac was snuggled in next to me on the couch as we watched TV. He was so peaceful lying with his nose snuggled in my hand. I rubbed his shoulders, hips, and tummy with the other hand. His silky, thick fur was so soft. I wanted to snuggle in even closer. As a pup, he would only take this kind of rubbing for a little while. Now I could have stayed there all night, and he would happily comply. If only those rubs could bring him complete healing. If only his submitting so deeply to my affection could bring him strength and that nasty tumor would go away.

Sometimes snuggling him, I think of losing him soon, and I have to swallow down tears. No need for those tears now. Our boy is still with us. "Be brave," I'd tell myself, "for today is not the day to say goodbye."

Epilogue

We did have to say goodbye to our beloved Mac. His strength and appetite began to wane that following April. I tried cooking him rice, chicken, steaks and feeding it to him by hand. Pretty soon, he refused all food and then passed within forty-eight hours. The cancer and the anti-inflammatory caused his liver to fail one year and a half after the diagnosis.

The morning before he passed, he went on the walk with us and carried his bumper proudly. I had to help him up inclines on the trail as he would stumble. In spite of this, he wanted to retrieve his bumper in the water like Molly and PJ were doing. I tossed it for him just in front of him. He grabbed it and seemed happy. That night, Mike laid out a sleeping bag for me, and I slept next to Mac, holding him close. I fell asleep but was awakened by his final breath at 2:00 a.m.

We had several memorials for him. The first was Mike and me by the pond at MacHaven. I made a wreath out of branches and flowers. We placed a tennis ball in the center with "Our beloved Mac" written on it, and we cut it open to place some of his ashes inside it. Mike and I stood on the shore and watched the wreath float out in the pond. It floated for several days before it sank. The second memorial was at the family cabin on Memorial weekend. I made a similar wreath, and Mike, Grace, and I paid tribute to our Mac.

We wrote and read the following for his memorial:

> In memory of Hiltonhall's Machias Burton, JH,
> our beloved Mac.

Born September 26, 2002, and brought to our home on Thanksgiving weekend, our wonderful bundle of fur, Mac. Russ called him butterball as he was yellow and well proportioned. Mac's heart and desire to please showed from the time he was a puppy who gleefully jumped into his crate at mealtime through his life in hunting and helping with chores, like when he carried the split wood from me to Jason (Mike's son) to be stacked and, in his last hunting season, he jumped out of the truck like Superman to save the day and found that duck the young ones couldn't find. He was a good companion, wanting to go everywhere with us. Everyone loved Mac as he was friendly and loved the attention. He would show off his toy or bumper and run with joy when spurred on with clapping.

Now you run joyfully without us, and we miss you terribly. But we take solace in knowing we will see you again and in remembering how you blessed us with your life.

We then put the wreath in the river he so loved to wade in and where he found sticks to pull up out of, and we watched it float down the river.

The third memorial was during hunting season following his passing at Linda Lake, where he had his first hunt and so many more. We prepared a basket of flowers with the tennis ball and some of his ashes and a purple ribbon (the color of his puppy ribbon). It was an overcast day, but as we set up our decoys, the sun broke out. Mike waded out with Mac's basket and set it in the lake. As his basket passed by, Mike, Steve, and I gave him a salute by shooting our shotguns once. *Bang!* Molly and PJ were off in the water after Mac's basket. I was concerned they would sink it. But once they nosed it, they turned and headed off toward the decoys. We finally got the dogs back in to shore, PJ with a decoy in tow. As I was untangling PJ, in came some ducks. *Bang!* Down one fell. Mike got one! Off went Molly. PJ tried to follow, but I was still untangling him. I got the last loop off his leg, and he was off. Molly was returning with the duck when PJ reached her. She let go of the duck, and PJ took over, bringing it into shore. Just then, another duck flew over, and Mike shot. It landed on its back and was struggling to get up. Molly was on the mark. Steve gave the duck another shot, and it became quiet. Molly snatched it and brought it to shore. They both got a retrieve. That was a great send-off to Mac!

We took comfort in these scriptures:

> And God said, "This is the sign of the covenant I am making between me and you and every living creature with you, a covenant for all generations to come: I have set my rainbow in the clouds, and it will be the sign of the covenant between me and the earth. Whenever I bring clouds over the earth and the rainbow appears in the clouds, I will remember my covenant between me and you and all living creatures of every kind. Never again will the waters become a flood to destroy all life. Whenever the rainbow appears in the clouds, I will see it and remember the everlasting covenant between God and all living creatures of every kind on the earth." (Gen 9:12–16)

> For the creation waits in eager expectation for the children of God to be revealed. For the creation was subjected to frustration, not by its own choice, but by the will of the one who subjected it, in hope that the creation itself will be liberated from its bondage to decay and brought into the freedom and glory of the children of God. We know that the whole creation has been groaning

as in the pains of childbirth right up to the present time. (Rom 8:19-22)

And this poem, "The Rainbow Bridge":

Just this side of heaven is a place called Rainbow Bridge.

When an animal dies that has been especially close to someone here, that pet goes to Rainbow Bridge. There are meadows and hills for all our special friends so they can run and play together. There is plenty of food, water, and sunshine, and our friends are warm and comfortable.

All the animals that had been ill and are old are restored to health and vigor. Those who were hurt or maimed are made whole and strong again, just as we remember them in our dreams of days and times gone by. The animals are happy and content, except for one small thing: they each miss someone very special to them who had to be left behind.

They all run and play together, but the day comes when one suddenly stops and looks into the distance. His bright eyes are intent. His eager body quivers. Suddenly he begins to run from the group, flying over the green grass, his legs carrying him faster and faster.

You have been spotted, and when you and your special friend finally meet, you cling together in joyous reunion, never to be parted again. The happy kisses rain upon your face; your hands again caress the beloved head, and you look once more into the trusting eyes of your pet, so long gone from your life but never absent from your heart.

Then you cross Rainbow Bridge together.

Air Mac, our all out boy.

Acknowledgments

I must first thank my husband, Mike, who is my best friend and love, who patiently supported me through this writing and encouraged me continually that I could do this. This book would not have happened if it were not for him. I also am very thankful for Chuck and Sharon Hilton and Cheri Wildes, who have given much time to us in helping us to be successful with Mac, Molly, and PJ in training, breeding, and health. They are wonderful examples of the Labrador community. Where would we be without Linda Rosellini-Burns? We are so thankful for the training, teaching, and support she gave us for Mac.

About the Author

Maurita Motland was born and has lived her life in the greater Seattle, Washington, area. She currently resides with her husband, Mike, in Enumclaw, Washington. After completing her bachelor of arts and science in voice performance at the University of Washington, she has worked various administrative positions. She has written many worship songs, which she performs in the churches she has been involved in. Maurita has always had a passion for writing and has recently been able to dedicate time to it. Her passion for her Labrador retrievers grows daily, and she continues to work to be their confident, loving pack leader relying on God's grace to get her there.

CPSIA information can be obtained
at www.ICGtesting.com
Printed in the USA
LVHW05s0718120418
573191LV00009B/34/P